CHURCH SIGNS

Seven Metaphors that Clarify the Mission of the Church

DAVID WILSON

LORENE WILSON

Copyright © 2024 by David and Lorene Wilson

All rights reserved, including the right of reproduction in whole or in part in any form, except for brief quotations in printed reviews, without prior permission of the publisher.

Except where noted, Scripture quotations are from The ESV® Bible (The Holy Bible, English Standard Version®), copyright © 2001 by Crossway. Used by permission. All rights reserved. All emphases added by author.

Publisher Information

Three Strand Partners

Kansas City, MO USA

For more information or to contact the author, please email: ThreeStrandPartners@gmail.com.

ISBN 978-0-578-16199-0 (softcover)

ISBN 979-8-218-41036-0 (eBook)

Cover design: Terry Dugan

Cover image: Rob Grace

Editorial team: Vickie Deppe, Marti Blankenship and Cristina Wright

Interior design: Ben Wolf, Inc.

Artwork used by permission.

Publishing services provided by BelieversBookServices.com.

First printing: 2024

Printed in the United States of America

CONTENTS

Acknowledgments	vii
Introduction	1
1. The Bride	12
2. The Body	30
3. The Branches	48
4. The Building	64
5. The Brothers and Sisters	82
6. The Bulwark	100
7. The Beacon	116
Conclusion	137
Appendix	141
Bibliography	143
About the Authors	145

We dedicate this book to our dear friend and benefactor Faythe Laatsch-Coley, whose questions about the mission of the church caused us to think more deeply than we ever had before.

ACKNOWLEDGMENTS

Within every church, some extraordinarily talented people possess untapped potential. This is true at Briarcliff Church in Kansas City, Missouri. We began attending in February 2023 after being without a church home for seven years. Our work within a missionary sending agency kept us busy visiting a different church every Sunday, so we indeed suffered a sense of homelessness for an extended season of our lives. Very shortly after meeting the family at Briarcliff, we realized we found our new home.

We were astonished that the Lord had prearranged so many things we had longed for in a local gathering of believers. During those years of wandering around the wilderness among the unchurched, the concept of this book was conceived. We yearned to find people who were thoughtful in their faith practice, so it was refreshing to find those who walked and talked like us. Briarcliff began a sermon series on our first visit called "Foundations of the Church," which was a study of the book of Acts. So much of what we were writing was echoed in that sermon series.

The next sermon series at Briarcliff was called "This is the Church," which took us on a deep investigation of the church at Ephesus. We sensed the Lord affirming the thoughts we'd expressed in our writing through the pastoral ministry of Tim, André and Vernon. They gave us permission to use an office in the building so we could put all of our focus on writing within the context of an active local body of Christ-followers.

Charlene, who has the spiritual gift of making connections, began introducing us to the amazing people who would lend their expertise to drafting this manuscript.

Marti retired a few years ago from the local seminary where she spent much of her time editing the writing of scholars and professors in an academic setting. We felt so honored when she agreed to review and proofread each chapter. She worked many wonders with her red ink pen!

Rob is an extraordinary artist who has turned his gift into a career, making the world a more beautiful place. We commissioned him to design the cover for our book, and we love how it turned out.

We are thankful for all of these people in this one little expression of Christ's body who have cared for us and encouraged us to complete the task that was assigned to us by the one who works all things "together for good, for those who are called according to his purpose" (Romans 8:28).

INTRODUCTION

Seven Metaphors that Clarify the Mission of the Church

The church is a mystery and a paradox, all wrapped up in a conundrum.

We are in a discovery process of trying to find the church. It seems to be hidden, buried deep under a pile of good intentions. Thankfully, there are seven signs pointing us to its concealed location. The New Testament writers described the church through seven metaphors as the Lord was revealing it to them:

1. **The Bride**: *"Husbands, love your wives, as Christ loved the church and gave himself up for her...."*   Ephesians 5:25
2. **The Body**: *"He gave the apostles, the prophets, the evangelists, the shepherds and teachers, to equip the saints for the work of ministry, for building up the body of Christ...."*   Ephesians 4:11
3. **The Branches**: *"I am the Vine; you are the branches."*   John 15:5
4. **The Building**: *"In him you also are being built together into a dwelling place for God by the Spirit."*   Ephesians 2:22
5. **The Brothers and Sisters**: *"For whoever does the will of my Father in heaven is my brother and sister and mother."*   Matthew 12:50
6. **The Bulwark**: *"... the church of the living God, the pillar and bulwark of the truth."*   1 Timothy 3:15 NRSV
7. **The Beacon**: *"You are the light of the world."*   Matthew 5:14

CHURCH SIGNS

Search for signs of the Church

After more than twenty-five years of serving on staff in local churches, we accepted a church engagement position for a missionary sending agency. After many years of being insiders in local churches, we suddenly became outsiders with the ability to choose our church home. Pastors rarely get the opportunity to visit other local churches, so this was a very revealing time for us. At first, it was exciting to get to know all the churches in our new community in the course of our work. However, after visiting more than seventy congregations, we simply could not decide to join any of them. They were all so different, each with their own strengths and weaknesses.

We went to small rural fellowships, inner-city congregations, mega-churches, and even local micro/house church gatherings. The small rural churches were very close-knit and family-oriented, but that made them a little less likely to reach out to strangers. Larger suburban churches were very focused on outreach, but their size made them less family-oriented. The inner-city churches tended to be very accepting of all people, but that meant they compromised their teaching to accommodate people with alternative lifestyles. The charismatic churches had rich and engaging times of prayer and worship, but they did not have an active global missions focus. Those churches with a dynamic global outreach and evangelistic push had the tendency to be project-oriented but struggled to develop deep and abiding relationships. Many churches focused on numbers to judge their success, particularly the house church movements. Each church had a unique strength, but they all seemed to overlook their weaknesses. Very few had a system of evaluating the fulfillment of their role and calling as the church of the living God.

Comparing and researching congregations became a passion for us. This was not only for our work but also for meeting our spiritual needs of fellowship, encouragement and accountability. After a while, the Lord impressed us to consider each church from his perspective. We asked the question, "What is the original design for the church according to the Scriptures?" Can we even compare the persecuted first-century church found in the New Testament to the "First Bapticostal Mennoterian Church" down the street? Did any of the churches in the New Testament have a name or a building with a sign on it? Is it okay to exchange the concept of "breaking of bread in their homes" (Acts 2:46) with "enjoying coffee and donuts in the lobby?" Can the biblical concept of "fellowship" actually happen in ninety seconds by greeting those seated around you? Is compromising truth an inevitable means to the goal of increasing church attendance?

These things may seem minor, but we were sincere in our desire to find a church that was earnestly seeking to reflect the description found in Scripture. We did not want to invest our lives in anything less than the *Bride of Christ*. We looked for signs of the *Body of Christ* that served the Lord by serving humanity and abiding in the vine as *Branches* that bear fruit for a Kingdom that is not of this world. We were not looking for a *Building* made with human hands, but we were seeking a gathering of saints called to be a living temple where the Holy Spirit dwells. Our goal was to find a group of people who long to be the family of Almighty God, *Brothers and Sisters* living together as a *Bulwark of Truth* under the protection of their heavenly Father, fortified from a world compromised by sin and deceit. We needed a gathering of people who understood their position in Christ and were eager to reflect his light as a *Beacon* in their neighborhoods and among the nations.

This search compelled us to examine these mysterious and paradoxical metaphors in the New Testament. It seemed to us that previous generations of church leaders read the Scriptures and instituted organizations that reflected not only their understanding of the church but also their own bias and cultural worldview. Over time, these local churches built layers of stuff that did not exist in previous generations. The next generation would seek to emulate what was passed down to them and then proceed to add more stuff. This continued generation after generation until the original was no longer recognizable and its current version became obscure, confusing and, quite frankly, obsolete.

To use computer language, some of the local churches we visited just needed a simple "reboot" while others needed a "hard reset" back to the original factory settings. The New Testament writers were writing the church's "operating system" when they used these seven metaphors, and it is the job of each generation to update the software when the hard drive gets corrupted by all of the malware that exists in the world. For those on the inside of church leadership, it is very difficult to see the glitches until there is a crash. Often, it takes an outsider to provide support and solutions for things insiders cannot see. We were outsiders for six years, and this book is the product of our quest to discover the original operating system of the church as the Lord intended.

Why do so many people avoid the church? Many of them are believers but have determined there is something fundamentally flawed in the church, so they stay away. Sometimes they say the institution is boring, irrelevant and meaningless. Others say the organization they experienced is too politically charged and distracted by things of the world. All of these things can be said of any institution that has lost its way in this world. By taking a step back and studying the original design of the church, we sought to unearth the remnants of the church that Jesus is building in our generation. We must remember:

The Lord is building (verb) his church. It is not a building (noun). It is a people! They are a gathered and scattered people for the sake of the gospel.

Pew researchers regularly conduct surveys to discover what people think about organized religion. According to their research, the fastest-growing segment of our population answers the question of "religious affiliation" as "none."[1] These "nones" are mostly spiritual but have decided there are too many problems with the church to get involved. Here are some of the conflicting ideals we discovered between the church as described in Scripture and the church culture that exists in our world today.

- **Individualism:** While the New Testament church was profoundly community-oriented, the North American church is hyper-individualistic just like the culture where it is found. Evangelicals frequently proclaim a gospel where individuals are encouraged to seek a "personal" relationship with God.
- **Consumerism:** The church that exists in our capitalistic economy is built upon competition by having bigger

---

[1]. "Nones" on the Rise, www.pewresearch.org/religion/2012/10/09/nones-on-the-rise/, accessed March 30, 2024.

buildings, better childcare services and more highly educated staffs than the church down the road; but the first-century church was focused on engaging and equipping the saints for sharing, giving and serving in their weaknesses.

- **Entertainment:** The average American television show is one hour for dramas and thirty minutes for sitcoms. Is that why most churches host one-hour worship services with thirty minutes of music? Does the church in North America allow Hollywood to influence their schedule and accommodate diminished attention spans? Are there any other subtle influences?

- **Narcissism:** Mega-churches are experiencing massive growth due to the charismatic personalities of celebrity pastors.[2] This is understandable in our culture since we idolize celebrities, politicians and business leaders who exhibit strong egos and command a powerful position of authority. This leadership style has built huge institutional churches, but this type of leader is a direct contradiction to the servant leader espoused in Scripture.

- **Institution:** Lastly, what about the institutional model of the church? Is that really what the New Testament describes? This book is not anti-institutional, but the question needs to be asked so that we can understand and work with all of its strengths and weaknesses.

For years, the institutional church has benefited from faithful research by thoughtful men and women who developed "bullet point" observations of church identity. Here are three we have chosen out of widely available dozens.

---

2. "Rise and Fall of Mars Hill" *Christianity Today*, www.christianitytoday.com/ct/podcasts/rise-and-fall-of-mars-hill, accessed March 30, 2024.

The Five Purposes of a Purpose Driven Church[3]

Pastor Rick Warren of Saddleback Church in California blessed the church with his five purposes of the church in 1995. Since then, church leaders around the world have used these five purposes to restructure and reinvigorate their congregations. These are tangible bullet points to help structure staff, budget and calendar, as well as assess strengths and weaknesses. Pastor Warren developed this as a practitioner, and it has served the institutional church well:

- Worship
- Teaching
- Fellowship
- Evangelism
- Serving

9Marks of a Healthy Church[4]

Like all institutions, the local church goes through seasons of growth and decline. Consultation groups like 9Marks have been established to "equip church leaders with a biblical vision and practical resources for building healthy churches." Their books and events highlight the nine marks of a healthy church:

- Expository Preaching
- Biblical Theology
- The Gospel
- Conversion
- Evangelism
- Membership
- Discipline
- Discipleship
- Leadership

---

3. Rick Warren, The Purpose Driven Church: Growth Without Compromising Your Message & Mission (Lake Forrest: Zondervan, 1995)
4. Mark Dever, 9Marks of a Healthy Church (Center for Church Reform, 2001)

INTRODUCTION

Foundations: Twelve Characteristics of a Church[5]

Local churches have recognized the enormity of Christ's Great Commission mandate to take the gospel message to all the world and have asked the question, "How do we reach the entire world and establish churches in vastly different cultures?" In response, mission societies were formed, beginning in the early nineteenth century to pioneer new work in "regions beyond" where the church does not exist. One of the largest and most influential missionary societies is the International Mission Board of the Southern Baptist Convention (IMB). The work of the IMB overseas has led them to publish a document called "Foundations" in which they define what a church looks like in any culture around the world, especially in places where Christianity is not welcome. According to the IMB, there are twelve biblical characteristics of a church in any context:

- Evangelism
- Discipleship
- Membership
- Leadership
- Preaching/Teaching
- Ordinances (Baptism & Communion)
- Worship
- Fellowship
- Prayer
- Accountability/Discipline
- Giving
- Mission

With all of these bullet-point descriptions of the church, we found ourselves informed but not inspired. Where is the mystery? Where is the paradox? A checklist is a great thing to have when we go to the grocery store! But can the New Testament church be reduced to an enumerated

---

5. "Foundations," International Mission Board, last modified June 10, 2022, accessed March 30, 2024, www.store.imb.org/imb-foundations

inventory of biblical concepts that are condensed for the sake of human comprehension?

One of the perspectives we bring to this conversation is from the global church. We have visited more than ninety countries, so our point of view blends the concept of a biblical church as it exists in the luxurious freedom of North America as well as those that survive in oppressive obscurity around the world. While searching for our own home church, we experienced a conundrum by straddling these two worlds. In the first world, we have street signs that mark the location of the church because it has been accepted and tolerated by the surrounding culture for centuries. But on the other side of the world where missionaries are working, a church cannot advertise and is often camouflaged for survival. We have found that, in either circumstance, the true signs of the New Testament church are not made of wood, steel or stone. They exist in metaphors so that believers everywhere can find their way to Christ and the church that he is building.

In each chapter, we will introduce you to various missiological concepts that missionaries use in foreign cultures as they establish churches that are both biblical as well as culturally relevant. Consider these tools to understand the culture outside of the church so that our leaders can make adjustments for a more faithful and impactful organization.

Mystery

In our age of enlightened reasoning and scientific methods, we are uncomfortable with mystery. We want to break things down into bite-sized, digestible pieces for ease of understanding. The primary reason we have an institutionalized church model is so we can make something that is uniquely heaven-centric more understandable for our earth-centric existence.

INTRODUCTION

Merriam-Webster defines *mystery* as "something not understood or beyond understanding: an enigma"[6] All these *purposes, characteristics* and *marks* we have mentioned can be found within the New Testament metaphors. Biblical authors knew the church is much more than we could ever understand or fully comprehend, so they wrote metaphorically to unveil the mysteries of God. These mysteries are so profound they could not be put into mere bullet points. We need to retrain our brains to be more comfortable with mystery, unresolved problems and incomplete...

(It bothers you that we didn't complete the sentence, doesn't it?)

Even the word *church* is somewhat of a mystery. In Greek, it is *ekklesia*, which conveys the idea of a gathering or an assembly of people for a common purpose. This was more of a secular term, and not necessarily a religious term like temple, synagogue or sanctuary. There are some places in Scripture where translators used a different word depending on the context, as in Acts 19:32, 41 where the biblical writer used ekklesia to describe a mob of rioters who had gathered for a demonstration (ESV translates it as "assembly"). Even though ekklesia is mostly translated as *church* in other places, we would never use the word church to describe a riot, right? Likewise, first-century readers would have never used the word ekklesia to describe a building or an institutional organization.

The word *church* on the building does not mean it is the church that Jesus is building!

---

6. Mystery, Merriam-Webster Dictionary (2002), www.merriam-webster.com, continuously updated, March 30, 2024.

Paradox

Jesus and His followers made frequent use of paradoxical thinking like:

"...whoever loses his life for my sake will find it."	Matthew 16:25
"...the last will be first, and the first last."	Matthew 20:16
"...whoever humbles himself will be exalted."	Matthew 23:12
"...when I am weak, then I am strong."	2 Corinthians 12:10
"...whatever gain I had, I counted as loss for the sake of Christ."	Philippians 3:7

Merriam-Webster defines *paradox* as "a statement that is seemingly contradictory and yet is perhaps true."[7] On the surface, paradox does not make sense, but the New Testament writers made these statements so believers would probe deeper into their meaning. This exercise in abstract thought can pierce the veil between heaven and earth and reveal the spiritual insight necessary to grow in our understanding of the church. Even though these statements describe paradoxical thinking for the individual believer, they can also be beneficially applied to the church as a collection of believers.

The Conundrum

Merriam-Webster defines *conundrum* as "an intricate and difficult problem having only a conjectural answer."[8] Some have asserted that we are entering a new era of the church where we likely will cease to be tolerated by the world around us—even in North America. We are not guaranteed freedom of religion tomorrow. If that is true for the church going forward, then we urgently need to get back to the basics. Church buildings may become a thing of the past, which is true in many countries around the world today. So, what does the church look like

---

7. Paradox, Merriam-Webster Dictionary (2002), www.merriam-webster.com, continuously updated, March 30, 2024.
8. Conundrum, Merriam-Webster Dictionary (2002), www.merriam-webster.com, continuously updated, March 30, 2024.

INTRODUCTION

when it does not have a street sign? Christians may not always have the freedom of speech. That also is true in many places around the world. So, what does the church sound like when it cannot speak publicly? The first-century churches were started during a time when they could not own property or build buildings. They were outlawed for proclaiming their faith in many places due to social and legal opposition. Yet the church increased and endured ***unhindered*** for the sake of the gospel. We want to see the church pursue the same thing the Apostle Paul experienced at the end of the book of Acts.

He lived there [Rome] two whole years at his own expense, and welcomed all who came to him, proclaiming the kingdom of God and teaching about the Lord Jesus Christ with all boldness and without hindrance.   Acts 28:30-31

This is not an attempt at "deconstruction," nor is it anti-institutional or end-times paranoia. When we highlight the worst-case scenarios of first-century persecution or end-times prophecy, it is to underscore the core essentials necessary for a triumphant and flourishing church in good times as well as times of crisis.

At the end of each chapter, you will find a list of questions that serve as a scoring exercise to help evaluate the strengths and weaknesses of your church's practice of each of the seven biblical metaphors we explore in this book. Then, in the appendix, you will find the scoring metric you can use to celebrate strengths as well as weaknesses that need to be addressed.

We are searching for the essential signs of the church according to Scripture. This investigation into the biblical metaphors of the church will seek to reveal the basics of a biblical New Testament church, so it can increase and endure for the sake of the gospel, no matter where it is planted. The message of hope can flourish with or without all the luxuries of the institution, the buildings and the freedoms many of us currently enjoy.

The church that Jesus is building is not a place or an activity; it is our identity as believers in Jesus Christ gathered and scattered around the world for the sake of the gospel.

I
THE BRIDE

This Church Sign brings clarity to the
church's mission of worship and prayer.

*Husbands, love your wives, as Christ loved
the church and gave himself up for her…*
Ephesians 5:25

Descriptions of the Church Exemplified by the Bride:

- Worship (Purpose Driven Church, IMB Foundations)
- Prayer (IMB Foundations)

"The bride of Christ" metaphor highlights the church's intimate relationship with our Lord. This is the vertical relationship between the Creator and his creation. There are a variety of passages that flesh out the church's spousal position with Christ as our groom-in-waiting. In this chapter, we want to dig deeper and discover the meaning behind the church as the bride. What is the essence of biblical history, and how can we make an application in modern church culture?

There is something mysterious and poetic about worship, which is why it is often equated with the arts: music, poetry, drama, sculptures, décor, tapestries, paintings and so much more. In preparation for writing this chapter, we spent some time interviewing worship pastors in local churches to ask both personal and professional questions about how they lead congregations to worship the Lord. We discovered most of them were not just musicians; they were actively engaged in a wide variety of right-brain activities and extraordinary creative artistry. They took their role far more seriously than just arranging music to match the message during the weekend services. They were seeking to reflect the beauty of our Creator through a variety of sensory means: visual, audible, touch, scent, speech, song and even a little bit of mystery. They all mentioned there is something special about adding the element of pause in between all of the other activities.

One worship pastor had a most vivid description of worship. He explained his goal was to create familiarity. He said,

> You know how it feels when you go to the barbershop or hair salon? You have an appointment, and you sit in the chair. The stylist begins by washing your hair to get it prepared for the trimming shears. Then she gets to work by shaping and trimming, all while others around you are experiencing the same thing. There is a familiar smell, and you are well-acquainted with the sounds of the salon. The stylist engages you in conversation about your life, and you feel comforted knowing someone has your undivided attention for a while. You notice your hair trimmings

cover the floor, and you feel just a little bit lighter, having shed something you didn't want to carry around anymore. The chair turns around, and you see yourself in the mirror. A reflection of yourself, not the same as others see, but it is a likeness.

That is what worship does for us. In corporate worship, we get a chance to assess our image in the presence of God and his people. Over time, we become more and more familiar with our Creator/Designer/Stylist. Sometimes we need just a trim and other times we need a complete makeover. Either way, our familiarity intensifies with the hope that we are reflecting God's character as he intended from the beginning. The more time we spend in his presence, the fonder we will grow. Through worship, we get to know each other, learn how to speak with each other (prayer), learn how to do things together (service), learn what we want each other to know (reading Scripture), what breaks each other's heart (lament) and learn what we each enjoy (celebrate).

One of the most important things on every bride's checklist before the wedding is getting her hair done. As a church, we are preparing ourselves for the union of the Groom (Christ) and the bride (his church), so we are becoming more familiar with these expressions of worship.

Worship is not just about the bride. The more important question for worship pastors is, "What does God receive when we worship?" We have heard church-growth experts suggest that church leaders should tailor their worship services to accommodate the preferences of participants. But how do they pair that with meeting the requirements of sacrificial praise for an Almighty God? If we are made in his image, how can our worship reflect his glory to him? Is there recognition in a service of worship that draws attention away from our needs and preferences and yields an intentional acknowledgment of God's purpose?

Exploring the bride metaphor is all about worship. It's not about the style of music, song choices, dramatic elements or décor in the worship space. It's some of that but so much more! We have continually asked the question, "What does God receive when we worship?" But we have yet to hear a fitting answer. There are a few clues hidden in this church sign of the bride, like our submission to the truth of the gospel, our acknowledgment of the presence of the Holy Spirit and our commitment to bear his fruit. In the absence of a complete answer to the question, perhaps the process of continually discerning what God desires in our worship is the goal of a good worship pastor. That should be the most earnest life-long pursuit for every believer. If we had a quick and easy answer, then worship pastors would not have to work so hard to discover the mystery of adorning the Lord's bride. And the bride of Christ is worth all the hard work they put into making her ready for her big day.

Ethnomusicology

Music alone does not equal worship, and yet music is intimately associated with all of our creativity as humans. Every culture on earth has its own style of music and many missionaries study ethnomusicology so they can wisely introduce worship to people through familiar cultural sounds, patterns, rhythms and performance modes. Even within our own culture, there are subcultures, and it is critical for worship pastors to study the church environment to adapt their worship style to fit like a missionary in a foreign context. When local music styles are considered, worship can eclipse the whims of personal preferences.

Music can make all the other elements of worship flow to escort the church into the presence of God. Here are a few things biblically, other than music, that exist under the umbrella of worship: giving, serving, preaching, reading scripture aloud, praying, repenting and lamenting.

One worship leader suggested that music is like "the mortar that holds all of the bricks of worship together." He uses it as a device to transition the congregation from their earthly existence into the presence of God. Music assists in bridging the gap between a believer's intellect and their emotions. It can serve as a tool with the power to touch the soul, deep inside. It simultaneously involves the brain and engages the spirit. When done well, it can affirm the church's theological convictions and challenge deeply held assumptions. Music in the midst of worship transcends our environment and gives us a brief glimpse of glory.

There will come a day when all of creation is united with its Creator as described in the book of Revelation. The bride (church) is finally prepared for her Groom (Christ), and the wedding party is invited to the marriage supper. All the temporal earthly things we find so comfortable will be stripped away. We will be surrounded by all the different nations, tribes and peoples of the world to worship our Lord in complete unity. But until that day, the church is in preparation mode, just like a bride who is getting ready for her big day. The practice of worship and the rehearsal of prayer is our primary task as the church, so we can learn to be in a right relationship with our God.

John: The Marriage of the Lamb

John the Revelator used the bride metaphor in his powerful end-times vision of the marriage between Christ and his transformed bride.

Then I heard what seemed to be the voice of a great multitude, like the roar of many waters and like the sound of mighty peals of thunder, crying out,
"Hallelujah!
For the Lord our God
the Almighty reigns.
Let us rejoice and exult
and give him the glory,
for the marriage of the Lamb has come,
and his Bride has made herself ready;
it was granted her to clothe herself with fine linen, bright and pure"—
for the fine linen is the righteous deeds of the saints.
And the angel said to me, "Write this: Blessed are those who are invited to the marriage supper of the Lamb." And he said to me, "These are the true words of God." Then I fell down at his feet to worship him, but he said to me, "You must not do that! I am a fellow servant with you and your brothers who hold to the testimony of Jesus. Worship God." For the testimony of Jesus is the spirit of prophecy.

Revelation 19:6-10

These last chapters of Revelation are the only place where the word *hallelujah* is found in the New Testament. All the other times it is used are in the book of Psalm. Many modern songs for worship use this word, so next time you hear it, remember it is both ancient and future. We are caught in the middle of what has happened and what will happen. The church as a gathered community has the opportunity to be a link in the chain of events that has happened and will happen, and it all has to do with worshipping our Creator.

Leading up to this passage in Revelation, the writer is describing the end of the end times. The unseen battle that we cannot see right now is being fought in full view of the Revelator. By the time we get to Revelation 19, the battle is won and there is rejoicing in heaven. The "bride has made herself ready." Her dress is radiant because of the practice of righteous deeds. Let's investigate the difference between good deeds and righteous deeds in this section.

Righteous Deeds vs. Good Deeds

"... his bride has made herself ready; it was granted her to clothe herself with fine linen, bright and pure"- for the fine linen is the righteous deeds of the saints.

Revelation 19:7-8

The Greek word translated here as righteous deeds is *dikaiosune*. This is not the same as good deeds (*kalos erga*). The two are often confused by readers of English translations. There is quite a contrast, and it should help us in our quest to discover things the church does in worship.

One of the passages of Scripture that is often confusing is Matthew's account of the Sermon on the Mount. When read in English, it seems like Jesus was contradicting himself, but understanding the original Greek will bring some clarity hopefully.

You are the salt of the earth, but if salt has lost its taste, how shall its saltiness be restored? It is no longer good for anything except to be thrown out and trampled under people's feet.

You are the light of the world. A city set on a hill cannot be hidden. Nor do people light a lamp and put it under a basket, but on a stand, and it gives light to all in the house. In the same way, let your light shine before others, so that they may see your good works and give glory to your Father who is in heaven.

Matthew 5:13-16 (Salt & Light)

The good deeds here are kalos erga. These are deeds done for an audience here on earth. Jesus is encouraging his followers to do things that will get the attention of other people as a witness for unbelievers. But just a few verses later in this same Sermon on the Mount, he draws a sharp contrast to how we should conduct ourselves with righteousness.

Beware of practicing your righteousness before other people in order to be seen by them, for then you will have no reward from your Father who is in heaven. Thus, when you give to the needy, sound no trumpet before you, as the hypocrites do in the synagogues and in the streets, that they may be praised by others. Truly, I say to you, they have received their reward. But when you give to the needy, do not let your left hand know what your right hand is doing, so that your giving may be in secret. And your Father who sees in secret will reward you.

Matthew 6:1-4

In this passage, the word *dikaiosune* (righteousness) is used—the same word used in Revelation 19 for the bride's fine linen dress. Righteous deeds, not good deeds, are to be done for our heavenly audience to see and approve—not our earthly audience.

There is a struggle that takes place in our local churches. Things that are seen get attention, but things that are unseen get neglected. This is true in the church, and it is also true in our personal lives. We know we need to be witnesses of the gospel to our friends, family, fellow students and co-workers, but we also need to study for the next test, prepare for the next presentation, visit a sick relative or take the dog for a walk.

The church spends a lot of time on ancillary things like funerals, feeding the poor, counseling, sports clubs, weddings, graduations, holidays and the list goes on. But how much time is consumed with these activities versus how much time is spent on practicing righteousness like prayer, worship and proclaiming the gospel? There are a great many things the church can do, which is why pastoral leaders need to understand the difference between good deeds and righteous deeds. Some may look at the above list and ask why we would question things like funerals. Are we seriously questioning whether or not the local church should be engaged in funerals?

Consider the time when Jesus had a harsh response to a follower wanting to attend a funeral. He said, "Follow me, and leave the dead to bury their own dead" (Matthew 8:22). From a pastoral perspective, that sounds cold, but, even here, Jesus is helping his followers distinguish between good deeds and righteous deeds.

We are clearly instructed to do both but for different purposes. Church leaders would do well to take a close look at three things as an exercise for introspection concerning church activities: the calendar, budget and photos. Use these to evaluate the balance between righteous deeds and good deeds as reflected by these aspects of church life. Are they in balance?

**The word church on the building
does not make it the bride of Christ.**

Paul: Worship in Truth

John the Revelator is not the only New Testament writer to make use of the bride metaphor. The Apostle Paul used this concept in his letters to churches as he encouraged them to see themselves as the bride of Christ.

I wish you would bear with me in a little foolishness. Do bear with me! For I feel a divine jealousy for you, since I betrothed you to one husband, to present you as a pure virgin to Christ. But I am afraid that as the serpent deceived Eve by his cunning, your thoughts will be led astray from a sincere and pure devotion to Christ. For if someone comes and proclaims another Jesus than the one we proclaimed, or if you receive a different spirit from the one you received, or if you accept a different gospel from the one you accepted, you put up with it readily enough. Indeed, I consider that I am not in the least inferior to these super-apostles. Even if I am unskilled in speaking, I am not so in knowledge; indeed, in every way we have made this plain to you in all things.

2 Corinthians 11:1-6

Paul considered himself the matchmaker, saying he was the one who betrothed the church in Corinth to the Lord. To understand the context of this bride reference in 2 Corinthians, we need to know Paul was the missionary who first brought the gospel message to the people at Corinth. This was his mission field for which he suffered through beatings, imprisonment, death sentences, shipwrecks, robbery and many other physical and spiritual battles. But despite all of this, the gospel was planted and a local gathering of believers was formed. After its formation, the believers began dividing over various issues, so Paul wrote 1 Corinthians to bring them back together. Subsequently, once those issues were resolved—some false teachers (accusers) entered the scene and began undermining Paul's work, the people whom he sarcastically called "super-apostles."

Therefore, 2 Corinthians was written to demonstrate how important the true gospel is and to take back his flock from those who tried to steal it away. He is using powerful imagery as a way to say, "These accusers are trying to steal another man's bride!"

The local church, which he formed, is so enigmatic that Paul had to use this temporal earthly analogy to bring them back into alignment. He explained in the previous chapter that they can only imagine this mystery of the church with their sinful and worldly minds. One day we will see it as it is, but he used these images to make a profound point. This is one of the reasons why Jesus spoke in parables, John spoke in dreams and visions, the prophets of old declared their warnings through stories, so Paul used the betrothed bride metaphor.

So, what is Paul's main point? What is he trying to explain that he could not say in plain language and bullet points? It has to do with those "super-apostles" who were preaching "another Jesus" (vs 4). Paul said to his flock, "I betrothed you to one husband, to present you as a pure virgin to Christ." This gives us a little better insight into why he used a bride of Christ analogy to help the church think about their intimacy with the Lord and not allow themselves to be seduced by an imposter.

Paul was wooing this wayward gathering of believers back to their first love—Christ—to whom they were betrothed. He warned them to not be led astray by some weak theology. He reminded them of how fragile a burgeoning relationship can be by saying they were betrothed to Christ as his bride.

Earlier in the letter he highlighted in 2 Corinthians:

1. We have this treasure contained in jars of clay. (4:7)
2. Our bodies are now just tents, but we will one day have a house built by God in heaven. (5:1)
3. Now we have to focus on our mission on earth, to bring reconciliation between God and man. (5:18)

This is the message Paul first brought to Corinth, but these false teachers were leading them away from the simplicity of that message by claiming Paul was not a true apostle. They even used his sufferings against him. He gave us that great reminder that, when we are weak, Christ is our strength. Paul boasted in his weakness for he knew that through all of his challenges to get the bride (the church) ready for her wedding day, there would be more challenges until we are fully reconciled with our Groom. That is why worship, not just music, is so important for the gathered church. By worshiping together, we declare our dependence on the Lord, for his provision of reconciliation between us and for celebrating the hope that is in us individually and corporately. Even in far-off distant places where public gatherings are not allowed, it is essential for the church to assemble in homes, factory floors or even under a tree to edify each other in culturally appropriate worship.

Paul: Worship in Submission

The Apostle Paul also used a husband-and-wife analogy in his letter to the Ephesians. In this letter, he was caught up in a rapturous vision

(Ephesians 3:4-6) as he was writing these descriptions of marriage and the Lord's relationship with His church.

Wives, submit to your own husbands, as to the Lord. For the husband is the head of the wife even as Christ is the head of the church, his body, and is himself its Savior. Now as the church submits to Christ, so also wives should submit in everything to their husbands.

Husbands, love your wives, as Christ loved the church and gave himself up for her, that he might sanctify her, having cleansed her by the washing of water with the word, so that he might present the church to himself in splendor, without spot or wrinkle or any such thing, that she might be holy and without blemish. In the same way husbands should love their wives as their own bodies. He who loves his wife loves himself. For no one ever hated his own flesh, but nourishes and cherishes it, just as Christ does the church, because we are members of his body. "Therefore, a man shall leave his father and mother and hold fast to his wife, and the two shall become one flesh." This mystery is profound, and I am saying that it refers to Christ and the church. However, let each one of you love his wife as himself, and let the wife see that she respects her husband.
Ephesians 5:22-33

Earlier in this Epistle, Paul said, "When you read this, you can perceive my insight into the mystery of Christ..." (Ephesians 3:4). Paul's very long sentences show he was in a moment of free association where many things came to his mind, but he wanted to communicate those mysteries as he stated "...that you, being rooted and grounded in love, may have strength to comprehend with all the saints what is the breadth and length and height and depth, and to know the love of Christ that surpasses knowledge, that you may be filled with all the fullness of God" (Ephesians 3:17-19). Paul used the husband-and-wife analogy to explain something infinite by using finite terms. Just as in the first century, the church today remains quite the enigma, so he was seeking to unveil and reveal the mystery that was given to him by the Lord.

For our ears as North Americans, hearing the word *submission* can be very unpopular, especially when we relate it to the relationship between husband and wife. Most seminaries, denominations, mission organizations and churches have had to debate and form conclusions of authority along the lines of complementarianism and egalitarianism. It is clear from the text and our understanding of first-century cultural norms that Paul was using this analogy of wives submitting to their husbands to demonstrate how we as the church should submit to the leadership of Christ our Lord. This is not to proclaim pure authoritarianism and abuse of authority but submission in terms of having the mantle of extending authority.

As a church, we have the authority of our Husband—Christ. We often look at the word submission through a negative lens but think of it this way: because of our submission, the Lord delegates His authority on earth to us. We are licensed, appointed, authorized and assigned to be his ambassadors.

When it relates to diplomacy, the ambassador of a nation is submitting to something greater than self. And with that submission comes great authority and responsibility to speak on behalf of a sovereign land. Our submission to the Lord Jesus Christ comes with awesome authority and responsibility for a kingdom not of this world.

Most of what we know about the church comes from the Apostle Paul and a few other New Testament authors, but, strangely, Jesus only used the word church (ekklesia) two times during his earthly ministry. Those few mentions carry enormous implications for our role as a faithful bride of Christ.

> *[Jesus asked] "Who do people say that the Son of Man is?" And they said, "Some say John the Baptist, others say Elijah, and others Jeremiah or one of the prophets." He said to them, "But who do you say that I am?" Simon Peter replied, "You are the Christ, the Son of the living God." And Jesus answered him, "Blessed are you, Simon Bar-Jonah! For flesh and blood has not revealed this to you, but my Father who is in heaven. And I tell you, you are Peter, and on this rock I will build my **church**, and the gates of hell shall not prevail against it. I will give you the **keys** of the kingdom of heaven, and whatever you **bind** on earth shall be **bound** in heaven, and whatever you **loose** on earth shall be **loosed** in heaven."*   Matthew 16:13-19

*[Jesus said] "If your brother sins against you, go and tell him his fault, between you and him alone. If he listens to you, you have gained your brother. But if he does not listen, take one or two others along with you, that every charge may be established by the evidence of two or three witnesses. If he refuses to listen to them, tell it to the **church**. And if he refuses to listen even to the **church**, let him be to you as a Gentile and a tax collector. Truly, I say to you, whatever you **bind** on earth shall be **bound** in heaven, and whatever you **loose** on earth shall be **loosed** in heaven."* Matthew 18:15-19

Keys

As a married couple, we have matching keys that we carry around: car keys, house keys, office keys and many others. Those keys represent things we have dominion over—control, responsibility, care and authority. We can lock the doors and close our homes to block access from outsiders. We can also unlock and open our home to visitors with the keys we carry. Those keys represent submission and authority that we both share, just like Christ shares his keys with his church.

When the church is in submission to Christ, he gives his church authority over things on earth (as they are in heaven). This means we have the ability to bind and loose. We have his authority, dominion, control and responsibility for the church and the world. He gave us keys to the kingdom of heaven here on earth, and we can use those keys through our practice of prayer and worship.

For the last 200 years, the Great Commission church in the modern mission era has been very busy roaming the earth, looking for open doors so we can spread the gospel. But why would we walk around our house, our car and our boat looking for an open door, when all along we are holding the keys that will let us in? We have keys! They may get a little rusty from time to time, but the church of the Living God has the ability to unlock these closed doors based upon the authority given to us by the Lord! We look at a world in need of the gospel message, but, unfortunately, churches get caught up in so many other things—

distractions that keep us from using the keys Christ has given to his bride.

Prayer that is strategic, focused and expectant is a powerful key. "The prayer of a righteous person has great power as it is working" (James 5:16). Through prayer, we are given an incredible gift of intimacy and communion with our Lord. Sometimes all we see is our limitations, but the bride of Christ, serving under the authority of her Groom in complete submission, holds the keys to lock and unlock any door! You can feel the difference when you visit a church that prioritizes prayer. They have an external focus that is contagious because they make evangelism part of the lifestyle and expectations for every member. They send and receive missionaries with joy and enthusiasm, which results in much fruit.

Paul: Bearing Fruit

One of the most difficult theologies in all of Scripture is the New Testament believers' relationship to the Law of God. Romans 7 is where Paul explained this difficult concept by drawing upon the marriage analogy once again. We do not live in a "theocracy" today as in the days of the early church, so this metaphor provides us with a useful tool to understand our position under grace and not under the Law.

Or do you not know, brothers—for I am speaking to those who know the law—that the law is binding on a person only as long as he lives? For a married woman is bound by law to her husband while he lives, but if her husband dies she is released from the law of marriage. Accordingly, she will be called an adulteress if she lives with another man while her husband is alive. But if her husband dies, she is free from that law, and if she marries another man she is not an adulteress.

Likewise, my brothers, you also have died to the law through the body of Christ, so that you may belong to another, to him who has been raised from the dead, in order that we may bear fruit for God. For while we were living in the flesh, our sinful passions, aroused by the law, were at work in our members to bear fruit for death. But now we are released from the law, having died to that which held us captive, so that we serve in the new way of the Spirit and not in the old way of the written code.
Romans 7:1-6

The book of Romans is a systematic treatise on salvation for both Jews and Gentiles. Paul spoke to both groups about the Law of Moses as well as our justification through faith. The primary reason for this use of a marriage illustration as it relates to the church in Rome is to underscore that we are saved in order that we may bear fruit. The Law was about restrictions in our activity: sin, food, cleanliness, avoidance of evil and so forth. But now that we are no longer married to the Law, that relationship died and we now belong to Christ "in order that we may bear fruit." So, our salvation is not about the avoidance of sin and going to heaven when we die; instead, we have been called to accomplish a mission through the church.

We love riding motorcycles. One of the first things to learn about riding on the streets is to look at where you want to go, not at what you want to avoid. It seems simple, but it is one of the hardest things to do. The principle is that wherever you look, you will naturally move in that direction. If there is a pothole in the road, don't look at it but focus on where you want to go to avoid it. This is true in sports as well. Most coaches remind athletes to "keep your eye on the ball." Drug and alcohol addicts know this principle also because they need to fill their lives with something else that will replace the void that is left by the object of their addictions.

In healthy churches, the proclamation of the Gospel of Christ is the focus—not adherence to the Law of Moses. If we focus on the Law, we will run into it every time. But if we focus on Christ, the Husband, we will be drawn toward him.

The Lord and his Kingdom are all about bearing fruit. But just like riding a motorcycle and trying to avoid the potholes, fruit is sometimes counter-intuitive and counter-cultural to what we know and think. If you were a "law keeper" in Paul's day, then you would question, "Why do we need to die to the Law? Why can't we just keep the Law along with adding on the 'bearing fruit' idea?" Paul used the marriage analogy, and the freedom that comes through dying to the Law, so that his hearers would know they cannot be married to "justification by faith" until their marriage to the Law is terminated.

As believers, we are bound to each other in the church. We are not saved to be an individual follower of Christ, but we were saved to bear fruit together. We can do so much more together than apart. This wisdom is understood around the world and throughout the ages.

- The whole is greater than the sum of its parts. (Aristotle)
- TEAM: Together Everyone Achieves More
- If you want to go faster, go alone; if you want to go further, go together. (African Proverb)

We are called to bear fruit *together*. It may be more difficult, and it may mean we have to work with difficult people, but, somehow, in God's plan it is better. Even though we can worship and pray in solitude, we are instructed to do so corporately. "And let us consider how to stir up one another to love and good works, not neglecting to meet together, as is the habit of some, but encouraging one another, and all the more as you see the Day drawing near"
(Hebrews 10:24-25).

The fruit of corporate prayer and worship will be manifest in ways that have no earthly explanations apart from the movement of the Lord's spirit in the midst of the church. It may be a mystery to some; those who pray with great expectations will see a great harvest.

Paradoxically, there is a difference between the biblical model of "bearing fruit" and the world's concept of "producing fruit." Churches, mission agencies, seminaries and other Christian organizations sometimes fall into the naïve business philosophy of outcomes and a performance-related, ends orientation —as if the fruit of God's vineyard comes as a result of our labor, the work of our hands or the outcome of our own efforts. Time and again throughout Scripture, we are encouraged and compelled to remain, abide and persist in an intimate relationship with the Lord; and through that enduring faith context, we will bear fruit. Not as a result of our work for God, but because of God's work through us.

Failure to understand this concept will eventually lead to burnout in pastors and other ministry leaders because spiritual fruit cannot be produced by mortal efforts. This kind of fruit comes from what God is doing in us not just what we are doing for him. A focus on outcomes is an obstacle to the work of the Holy Spirit because it carries no power to change or transform lives, only a drivenness to produce results. Measuring tangible results is just another form of the Law with its incessant and legalistic restrictions.

When the church focuses on prayer and worship, it receives the keys that Jesus provides to his bride. With these keys, the church has the privilege to "bind and loose" anything that is under his authority—and *all* things in heaven and on earth are under his authority (Matthew 28:18). Until the day of the Marriage Supper, the bride is to make herself ready in the neighborhoods and among the nations. As the church remains faithful to Christ, it will bear fruit, not as the outcome of any good deed, but as a result of abiding in righteousness, just as a bride waiting for her Groom.

The Lord is building (verb) his church.
It is not a building (noun). It is a people!
They are a gathered and scattered
people for the sake of the gospel.

Scoring Metric for **The Bride**

This is the first of seven exercises to help your church evaluate strengths and weaknesses according to its practice of the seven biblical metaphors we explore in this book. Answer the questions below with a rating of 1-5. Add the results together and then divide by 5 to get the score for this chapter on worship and prayer. Record your results in the appendix to help you evaluate your congregation's strengths and weaknesses.

On a scale of 1-5:   Score

1. How well does your church represent the Bride of Christ in your town? _____
2. Is worship music consistent with the cultural modes of the community? _____
3. Does worship include submission to God with opportunities for sacrifice? _____
4. Is the practice of prayer honoring to the God of all creation? _____
5. Do you see fruit as the result of prayer being used as a key to open doors? _____

                                                                                             Total: _____
                                                                                             ÷ 5 = _____

(Record this number in the Appendix next to **The Bride**)

2
THE BODY

This church sign brings clarity to the church's
mission of serving, giving and leadership.

*He gave the apostles, the prophets, the evangelists, the shepherds and
teachers, to equip the saints for the work of ministry, for building up the
body of Christ ...*
Ephesians 4:11

Descriptions of the Church Exemplified by the Body:

- Leadership (IMB Foundations, 9Marks)
- Giving (IMB Foundations)
- Serving (Purpose Driven Church)
- Ordinances of Baptism and Communion (IMB Foundations)

A few years ago, a virus entered my body. It was so small that it couldn't be seen with the naked eye. I don't know where I picked it up or where it went when it was finished with me. This extraordinary, microscopic, inconvenient bug disrupted my life. It affected my sleep, my daily activities, the food I ate, my interactions with friends and family and my work. It also had major effects on our community, our nation and the world. This virus disrupted our economy, our political systems, our religious activities and our total sense of safety and well-being. Without mentioning its name, you know exactly what I am talking about.

Isn't it strange to reflect on such a small thing as a virus entering our bodies and how much of an impact it made on the world as we know it? Wouldn't it be great if, instead of a virus that brought us so much pain, there could be something that inhabits us that would bring us healing, love, joy and hope?

After the ascension of Jesus from his earthly ministry, he promised us his Holy Spirit who would indwell us to continue the mission he started,

You, however, are not in the flesh but in the Spirit, if the Spirit of God dwells in you. Anyone who does not have the Spirit of Christ does not belong to him. But if Christ is in you, although the body is dead because of sin, the Spirit is life because of righteousness. If the Spirit of him who raised Jesus from the dead dwells in you, he who raised Christ Jesus from the dead will also give life to your mortal bodies through his Spirit who dwells in you.

Romans 8:9-11

According to the Scriptures, Christ entered our world and took on a physical body. He demonstrated the love of God clearly, tangibly and boldly with power from on high by way of miracles, compassion and ultimately a demonstration of victory over death itself.

The work of our Lord Jesus is continuing today in the world through those whom he has called according to his purposes (Romans 8:28). The church, which is identified as his body in multiple passages throughout the New Testament, is the earthly representative of the continuing work of Jesus.

Members of the body of Christ are the physical ambassadors of Jesus in this world. This is the means through which Christ makes his message known in the world. Those members are indwelt by the Holy Spirit who gives them strength, power and a diversity of gifts in order to accomplish his mission (Romans 8:9). These members form the body and Christ serves as the head.

Mystical

Sometimes in English, we use the word body to describe a gathering or a group that has assembled for a common purpose like legislative bodies, civic bodies and even celestial bodies. This is known as a "moral body." But we will see in our Scriptures that there is something deeper and more profound when it is used to describe the church.

Some have interpreted the term *body of Christ* mystically. In Catholic and Orthodox teaching, the mystical body of Christ is said to be present in the Eucharist. They espouse doctrines on substance like transubstantiation or consubstantiation.

For Baptists, Pentecostals, and other Protestant traditions, there are two primary ordinances: Baptism and Communion (the Lord's Supper). They are meant to remember the work of Christ during his earthly ministry. In baptism, we are uniting with him symbolically by being buried (going under the water) and being raised again to new life. Communion, likewise, teaches us to remember his sacrifice on the cross, when his body (the bread) was broken, and his blood (the wine) was spilled for the forgiveness of our sins.

Some Anabaptists (Brethren, Mennonite, Apostolic Christian, etc.) also add head-covering and foot-washing practices to the list of ordinances. Still others embrace historic European traditions and observe six ordinances: Baptism, Communion, Preaching, Scripture Reading, Prayer and Singing.

If you explore a variety of church traditions, you will notice Protestants refer to these practices as ordinances, but our Catholic and Orthodox brothers and sisters use the word *sacrament*. Catholic traditions list seven sacraments: Baptism, Eucharist (Communion), Confirmation, Penance, Anointing of the Sick, Marriage and Holy Orders. In addition to Baptism and Communion, our Orthodox friends have an indefinite number of sacraments that include prayer, singing, service, procession and other events of blessing that help render the presence of God more tangible in the world.

The historical development of the words ordinance and sacrament is interesting. The New Testament was originally written in Koine Greek, so the original word we are discussing is *Mysterion* from which we derive the English word *mystery*. When the Scriptures were translated into Latin, they used the word *sacramentum* or sacrament. During the Protestant Reformation, the word sacrament had too much baggage and negative connotations attached to it, so, in English, they discarded the word and exchanged it for ordinance. Protestants also eliminated the long list of activities and decided to focus on just Baptism and Communion for greater clarity. The words *rites* or *rituals* will also appear in many churches.

This is not exhaustive, and the history is very complex, so our goal is to clarify and simplify this important topic. One of the premises in this book is that the church is a mystery, but being mystical is not one of our conclusions here. Whatever the church calls these activities, their main purpose is to demonstrate something mysterious by tangible demonstrations of grace and blessing to participants.

Mystery

Mystery is frequently used to describe, not a matter that is hard to understand, but one that has been concealed. When it is finally revealed, it can sometimes be difficult to believe due to our own biases, prejudices or worldviews. In our opinion, one of the biggest mysteries as it relates to the church being the Body of Christ is the question, "Why the church?"

Wouldn't it be way more effective to reach a world in need of salvation by just calling elite motivational speakers (like the prophets) who can demonstrate powerful miracles as evidence to the masses just like in the Old Testament? Why does God call average ordinary people from all walks of life to represent him in a broken and messy assembly like the New Testament local church? And yet, that is exactly what we are called to do: to equip, empower and deploy imperfect people with an essential message to remote places around the world. This is one of the most confusing mysteries of the church.

One of the greatest obstacles to the gospel message being broadly cast is the *myth of the preacher.* This is not to say that preachers do not exist but that the role sometimes keeps people with other gifts in the church from being actively engaged in proclamation. The word *preacher* comes from the concept of a "town herald" or person who makes proclamations in the town square. It only appears in the New Testament three times. Twice, Paul refers to himself as a preacher in his letters to Timothy, and the third is in Acts describing Paul's unfortunate reputation as a "preacher of foreign divinities" (1 Timothy 2:7; 2 Timothy 1:11; Acts 17:18). The common concept of hiring a professional herald in the church then deploying all the members to bring their friends, neighbors, family and coworkers to come and hear the preacher is not the model for the church as presented in the New Testament!

The word church on the building does not make it the body of Christ.

Encourage, Edify and Equip

The local church is a body of believers who have a variety of gifts, skills, talents and abilities that can be used to edify and encourage each other. Church leaders are tasked with the role of being equippers so members of the body are deployed to do the work of ministry in their neighborhoods and among the nations (Ephesians 4:4-16).

The myth of the preacher is critical to highlight because we see its abusive cycle in local churches everywhere. It starts innocently with a very gifted public speaker who gathers a crowd and develops a strong following. The method of evangelism that naturally follows is "come and hear our preacher." That is strangely reminiscent of the Old Testament concept of "come and see" to worship God at his temple in Jerusalem.

But Jesus was clear in all of the Great Commission passages that the "come and see" method has been exchanged for the new and improved "go and tell" method. His final instructions to his followers were to "go," "make disciples," "baptize," "teach," "proclaim," "to all nations," "in all the world," "to the ends of the earth," "until the end of the age" (John 20:21; Mark 16:15; Matthew 28:18-20; Luke 24:44-49; Acts 1:7-8).

All followers of Christ are given the privilege and honor to bear witness and proclaim the good news of the gospel. Romans 10:14 describes the activity of preaching but not the position or role of a preacher. Paul gave a list of titles for church leaders like pastors, elders, apostles, prophets and teachers, but the role or office of a preacher (proclaimer or herald) does not appear. Instead, he described individual giftings from the Holy Spirit who indwells believers to enable them to perform functions necessary for local church governance.

For as in one body, we have many members, and the members do not all have the same function, so we, though many, are one body in Christ, and individually members one of another. Having gifts that differ according to the grace given to us, let us use them: if prophecy, in proportion to our faith; if service, in our serving; the one who teaches, in his teaching; the one who exhorts, in his exhortation; the one who contributes, in generosity; the one who leads, with zeal; the one who does acts of mercy, with cheerfulness. Romans 12:4-8

Many great resources describe the biblical qualifications for church leaders like elders, bishops, overseers, pastors, deacons and more. The Scriptures provide a very simple and detailed list in 1 Timothy, Titus and 1 Peter. These passages highlight the characteristics of the leader, their duties and function within the body, as well as their calling to that role. But their primary function can be summed up in one simple phrase from Ephesians 4 "to equip the saints for the work of ministry." We are all called to be witnesses, but not everyone is called to be an evangelist, or a prophet, or a teacher or a shepherd. Some are better communicators than others. The ability to craft relevant messages, speak clearly, tell compelling stories, relate with the audience and challenge people to live their lives for Christ is a great ability. But it doesn't mean their gift is any more important than all the other gifts.

Gift Envy

Gift-envy and *gift-projection* are terms used by many evangelical leaders like Rick Warren to describe the desire to have a different gift from the one you have been given. For some evangelical believers, the gift of evangelism is envied and given an elevated status. Christ followers in this tradition can sometimes feel guilted into believing that all of the other gifts are inferior like mercy, giving, exhortation and service. You have probably seen churches host classes and training events for evangelism, but rarely will you see training in mercy. We see this gift envy in other protestant groups as well. Pentecostal and charismatic groups will often overemphasize miraculous gifts like tongues, prophesy and healing. Any group can fall prey to the temptation to emphasize perceived greater gifts according to their own doctrine and practices.

In 1 Corinthians, Paul was battling a stiff-necked church with lots of resistance from within and from their surrounding culture. Unity was a high value for Paul in all of the churches he established. In chapters 12-14, he was helping this stubborn Corinthian church see the value in each other in the midst of competing ideals. Just as in our churches today, they were experiencing gift envy. Consequently, Paul employed the use of the metaphor that the church is "one body" and all the members are important and necessary.

For just as the body is one and has many members, and all the members of the body, though many, are one body, so it is with Christ. For in one Spirit we were all baptized into one body—Jews or Greeks, slaves or free—and all were made to drink of one Spirit.

For the body does not consist of one member but of many. If the foot should say, "Because I am not a hand, I do not belong to the body," that would not make it any less a part of the body. And if the ear should say, "Because I am not an eye, I do not belong to the body," that would not make it any less a part of the body. If the whole body were an eye, where would be the sense of hearing? If the whole body were an ear, where would be the sense of smell? But as it is, God arranged the members in the body, each one of them, as he chose. If all were a single member, where would the body be? As it is, there are many parts, yet one body.

The eye cannot say to the hand, "I have no need of you," nor again the head to the feet, "I have no need of you." On the contrary, the parts of the body that seem to be weaker are indispensable, and on those parts of the body that we think less honorable we bestow the greater honor, and our unpresentable parts are treated with greater modesty, which our more presentable parts do not require. But God has so composed the body, giving greater honor to the part that lacked it, that there may be no division in the body, but that the members may have the same care for one another. If one member suffers, all suffer together; if one member is honored, all rejoice together.

Now you are the body of Christ and individually members of it. And God has appointed in the church first apostles, second prophets, third teachers, then miracles, then gifts of healing, helping, administrating, and various kinds of tongues. Are all apostles? Are all prophets? Are all teachers? Do all work miracles? Do all possess gifts of healing? Do all speak with tongues? Do all interpret? But earnestly desire the higher gifts. And I will show you a still more excellent way.

1 Corinthians 12:12-31

If you have surrendered your life to Jesus as the Lord of your life, then the Spirit of God dwells within you and has given you a gift to share in the church for the benefit of the body. What is your gift, and how can it be used to edify others within the body of Christ?

You may have the gift of mercy, for instance, and your church has a vibrant ministry to people who are suffering in some way. You just may be the answer to someone's prayer for help. Alternatively, if your church does not have a ministry to help people who are hurting, they may be open to starting one. It could be that they have been waiting for someone with your gift to join and make the body whole.

Recognizing your gift and exercising it with purpose is greater than just experiencing happiness or achievement individually. We are placed on earth to fulfill God's purposes, and we do that through community in the body he designed called the church. The Christian life is not about me but we.

Me to We

When Jesus said to Peter in Matthew 16:18, "… on this rock I will build my church …," he instituted the organizational plan to take people from being "me focused" to "we focused." Paul echoed that plan when he wrote, "For in one Spirit we were all baptized into one body"
(1 Corinthians 12:13). The Christian life is not meant to be lived alone. We were born again to live collectively for the sake of a kingdom not of this world. Our life now has a purpose to live for the collective whole and for the benefit of the whole world. If this sounds communistic, it has some of the same features. Listen carefully to the ideals espoused by earthly communism, and it will sound like what we know of the early church and even heaven itself.

And they devoted themselves to the apostles' teaching and the fellowship, to the breaking of bread and the prayers. And awe came upon every soul, and many wonders and signs were being done through the apostles. And all who believed were together and had all things in common. And they were selling their possessions and belongings and distributing the proceeds to all, as any had need. And day by day, attending the temple together and breaking bread in their homes, they received their food with glad and generous hearts, praising God and having favor with all the people. Acts 2:42-47

The problem with earthly communism is sin. It is the human condition that makes communism on earth impossible. It is a warped and twisted distortion of Christian values that has a semblance of truth but results in error. The Christian economist says, "Everything I have is yours," but communism says, "Everything you have is mine." We are encouraged by the Apostle Paul to keep striving to make the "we" a priority. We must see the value in each other, engage each other, hold each other accountable and, for leaders, equip all of the members to share ministry *in* the church and *through* the church.

Giving, Serving and Using your Gifts

Gallup is a global analytics and advice firm that helps churches and other organizations assess their strengths and weaknesses. Years ago, they developed a survey called the ME25, a Member Engagement Survey for faith communities consisting of 25 items.[1] It is designed to measure how church engagement impacts the lives of individual members. There are three areas of involvement: volunteering, connecting socially and decision-making. The results all prove the point that the Apostle Paul was making in his letter to the believers in Corinth 2,000 years ago. The survey results demonstrate a dramatic benefit for church members who were more than just weekend worship attendees.

---

1. Gallup (2015). *Member Engagement 25 survey results* retrieved from www.gallup.com/me25/.pdf

The data showed that engaged church members are:

- More than ten times as likely to invite someone to participate in their congregation.
- Nearly three times as likely to say they are extremely satisfied with their lives.
- Likely to spend more than two hours per week serving and helping others in their communities.
- Likely to give three times more to their faith communities annually.[2]

Giving, Serving and Discipleship

Churches of all sizes and denominations have discovered the benefits of this research and are seeking to get everyone involved in the work of the body in their neighborhoods and among the nations. Many have seen a direct connection between giving, service and discipleship.

As a child, I remember sitting in a church service and watching the offering plate being passed. I asked my mother what that money was for, and she said, "We are giving that money to God." In my simple and naïve mind, I imagined the pastor physically handing God the money in that collection plate. That is a special memory I want to hold on to—the sense that my gifts are not for an institution, a building or some activity, but that I am giving directly to my Lord. A few recent practices have made the act of giving to the Lord a little less satisfying. One of them is online giving. It is convenient and necessary, and it is a new way forward, but somehow the church needs to make that act more worshipful than just sending a receipt or a canned thank-you note. Let's make giving worshipful again by telling the story of where our giving goes and how the Lord is using our gifts to expand his kingdom here on earth. Giving and serving are equally important for a church to thrive, so think creatively and discover some ways to bring back a childlike faith to bridge the gap between heaven and earth.

---

2. www.Gallup.com, ME25 (Accessed April 25, 2023)

One of the best practices of effective churches is helping believers find the right fit for their service opportunities. It is not good to just involve people in any position that meets a need of the institution. For example, every church needs volunteers in their children's ministry. If you have spent any time at all in the institutional church, you have heard the pleas for adults to volunteer their time serving the kids. Recently, a church in our area sent out a request for volunteers, and some friends of ours responded. After the background check and an initial interview, the Director of Children's Ministry asked, "Why are you interested in volunteering?" They replied, "Well, mainly because you said there was a big need for volunteers." A second question was asked, "What kind of experience, skills and gifts do you have working with children?" Their honest answer was, "Not much; we just want to help." Our friends told us that was the moment they knew they were "a foot trying to do the work of a hand." Their story got us thinking about the body of Christ a little more pragmatically.

This church leader was very wise to guide them to serve in an area of the church where their gifts, talents and abilities could be better used. Not every church thinks this way. Some may think, "Hey, these people are volunteering, so we should let them do what they think they want to do." The unfortunate outcome is almost always burnout. Imagine if you lost the use of your hands, and you tried to do everything your hands once did with your feet: signing your name, brushing your teeth, driving, scratching behind your ear or whatever else. It is not only ineffective, but it will certainly lead to frustration. That is not the best way to lead the church, and it will show over time. However, Paul said he was showing us "a more excellent way."

There are lots of resources for the church to help congregants discover the gifts and strengths the Lord has given them. A wise church leader would do well to make the discovery process a top priority. Someone needs to be the champion of getting people properly engaged in the work of the church. It could be a "Discover your Design" class or simply an orientation gathering, but this needs to be done regularly, intentionally and proactively.

The traditional model of the church in North America—with its need to keep the institution alive—is often counter-productive. There are better ways of thinking about the church body, but there are no perfect ways. Many creative leaders are pioneering models like micro church, cell church, home church or simple church, and many others fall under the umbrella category of Disciple Making Movements (DMM). While not for everyone, they seem to be experimenting with some of the right ideas. For leaders in the institutional church (sometimes referred to as a legacy model or predominant model), it is worth at least a cursory investigation to see if there is wisdom to be gleaned and practices to be adapted.

Maturity is the Goal

Service and engagement in the church are not just good suggestions so congregants can feel better about themselves. There is something much deeper at stake. Paul used the body metaphor once again in his letter to the Ephesians to help them understand the roles of leadership in the church (teachers, pastors, etc.). The leader's job is not to do the work alone but to equip all the members of the body of Christ so they can share in the work of ministry. When these saints are equipped and deployed in ministry, they will grow in discipleship and maturity in Christ.

There is one body and one Spirit — just as you were called to the one hope that belongs to your call — one Lord, one faith, one baptism, one God and Father of all, who is over all and through all and in all. But grace was given to each one of us according to the measure of Christ's gift....

And he gave the apostles, the prophets, the evangelists, the shepherds and teachers, to equip the saints for the work of ministry, for building up the body of Christ, until we all attain to the unity of the faith and of the knowledge of the Son of God, to mature manhood, to the measure of the stature of the fullness of Christ, so that we may no longer be children, tossed to and fro by the waves and carried about by every wind of doctrine, by human cunning, by craftiness in deceitful schemes. Rather, speaking the truth in love, we are to grow up in every way into him who

is the head, into Christ, from whom the whole body, joined and held together by every joint with which it is equipped, when each part is working properly, makes the body grow so that it builds itself up in love.
Ephesians 4:4-7, 11-16

Part of our research for a Doctor of Ministry degree was developing a short-term mission trip training guide. We called it, "Transforming Missionaries." The study required real-world experiments to defend our thesis that "short-term trips help participants grow in their faith."[3] So, we sought several church leaders to participate in the experiment, which included pre-trip surveys and post-trip, follow-up surveys. We also had a control group during the same timeframe with the same questionnaire, but they did not go on a short-term trip. Their only activity was being actively engaged in small group Bible study and disciple-training classes. At the end of the survey phase of the research, we randomly selected some participants in both groups for face-to-face interviews. We wanted to see what made a deeper impact in their spiritual lives—the short-term mission trip or Bible study alone.

We had a very robust survey that asked a multitude of questions, but one subject produced some very surprising results. The question was, "On a scale of 1-5, how often do you pray?" We had over 160 participants, representing twelve different congregations. The initial results were all equal between the two groups. However, the post-experiment results were quite different.

The Bible-study-only group increased their estimated evaluation of their prayer life, but the mission trip participants showed a decrease in their assessment of time in prayer. Of course, on the surface, this result negated our thesis and caused us to reevaluate our initial assumptions. Once we started the in-person interviews, a clearer picture began to form as to the cause of this perceived decrease in prayer for mission trip participants.

The Bible study participant group grew steadily in their commitment to a consistent prayer time because they talked about it in their group, held each other accountable and reinforced the positive changes in their

---

3. David and Lorene Wilson, Transforming Missionaries: A Short-Term Mission Guide (Buies Creek, NC 2007)

lives every week as they met. Our interviews with these participants in the control group showed a definite benefit of maintaining a constant time of fellowship and Bible study along with accountability.

The short-term mission trip participant group had a very different experience. They all traveled for one or two weeks, experienced a different culture, interacted in a different language, ate different foods, worshiped in a different style of church and met people who lived in different socio-economic conditions. During our interviews, we asked these participants why they provided the numbers in both the pre-survey and post-survey for prayer. Specifically, "Why did you score lower after your mission trip?" Richard (a representative participant) said, "When I went to El Salvador, I saw the faith and prayer life of the people, and I realized that their devotion to the Lord is vastly greater than mine. When I get sick here at home, I go to the doctor. When they get sick, they pray for healing. When I get hungry, I open my refrigerator. When they get hungry, they pray for the Lord to provide. I realized my prayer life is nowhere near what it should be compared to their prayer life."

This was a very profound conclusion, and it gave us a great deal of hope for Richard and others who were able to assess their spiritual condition by comparison and contrast to others around the world. This is one of the most important benefits of an active short-term mission trip ministry in the local church.

Whether you are serving locally or globally, your effectiveness in the body of Christ is enhanced through your service. We all have a role to play in God's kingdom, so your first step is to find what you were created to do and do it with all your heart, soul, mind and strength in the context of the local body of the church where the Lord leads you to join (Mark 12:30).

There is an intimate bond between Christ as the head and the church as the body. As the human body is influenced, directed and governed by the head, so the church (the whole body of believers) is influenced, directed and governed by Christ. Unfortunately, there is the 80/20 dilemma. Twenty percent of the people do eighty percent of the work. We love that holy twenty percent! They deserve recognition at every opportunity possible, not just for their service, but also to inspire others to think differently about their involvement in the body. When a church regularly shines a light on the role models and positive examples from within the congregation, it gives the "eighty percenters" an indication that more is expected of them. Members of the body of Christ, just like parts of the human body, tend to atrophy, grow weak and waste away when they cease to be exercised.

Our pastor mentioned recently, "There are too many warts on Christ's body! Some people just attach themselves to the church but never contribute to the function of the church. What good is a wart?"

Without servants, givers and leaders using their unique gifts, the church will limp like someone who is missing a leg or lack dexterity like someone who is missing an arm. Without the participation of the "ear," how will the church hear the groans of prisoners who long to be set free (Psalms 102:20)? Without the "eye," how can we see those who are searching for hope? Whatever your gift, you are necessary for the body of Christ to be complete. As a believer, you have already received the gifts of the Holy Spirit and are inhabited by his power and direction. May the Lord bless you as you connect to his body, the church.

The Lord is building (verb) his church.
It is not a building (noun). It is a people!
They are a gathered and scattered
people for the sake of the gospel.

Scoring Metric for **The Body**

This is the second of seven exercises to help your church evaluate strengths and weaknesses according to its practice of the seven biblical metaphors we explore in this book. Answer the questions below with a rating of 1-5. Add the results together and then divide by 5 to get the score for this chapter on serving, giving and leadership. Record your results in the appendix to help you evaluate your congregation's strengths and weaknesses.

On a scale of 1-5:   Score
1. Is there a leadership team that is functioning as prescribed by Scripture? _____
2. Are the church leaders equipping the saints for ministry? _____
3. Are members giving sacrificially so the church is self-sustainable? _____
4. Does the church practice the ordinances of baptism and communion? _____
5. Is there specific training for all the members to use their unique gifts? _____

                                                                    Total: _____
                                                                    ÷ 5 = _____

(Record this number in the Appendix under the heading **The Body**)

THE BODY

3
THE BRANCHES

This Church Sign brings clarity to the church's
mission of evangelism and propagating the gospel.

I am the Vine; you are the branches.
John 15:5

Descriptions of the Church Exemplified by the Branches:

- Evangelism (9Marks, Purpose Driven Church, IMB Foundations)
- The Gospel (9Marks)
- Conversions (9Marks)

The possibility exists that there are more Christ followers in China than in North America! In 2018, the Chinese government released a census report that forty-four million known Christians were living in China.[1] Of course, because of persecution and fear of government oppression, these numbers only reflect those who confessed their faith. There are certainly many others who live in secrecy. Some international Christian organizations estimate tens of millions more, but it is very difficult to track the number of underground church members. There is gospel proclamation taking place, and people are being saved through active evangelism.

In another surprising statistic, the fastest-growing church is in Iran! Open Doors estimates there are between 800,000 and 1,250,000 Christ-followers in Iran.[2] Again, the numbers are difficult to verify due to fear of persecution. Much of this growth comes from prisoner conversions and women. Both groups are highly oppressed in Iranian society.

When believers hear the gospel in a relevant way, they tend to share their newfound faith, which leads to the propagation of the message among people living in similar circumstances. It may seem counterintuitive for growth to occur in the presence of hardship, but that is the natural order of life here on earth. Jesus highlighted this natural order one day as he taught his disciples about life through the metaphor of branches in a vineyard as it is recorded in the Gospel of John.

---

1. www.scio.gov.cn accessed on (March 25, 2024)
2. Interview by Justice.gov, 20 February 2020, cited on www.opendoors.org (accessed March 25, 2024)

I am the true vine, and my Father is the vinedresser. Every branch in me that does not bear fruit he takes away, and every branch that does bear fruit he prunes, that it may bear more fruit. Already you are clean because of the word that I have spoken to you. Abide in me, and I in you. As the branch cannot bear fruit by itself, unless it abides in the vine, neither can you, unless you abide in me. I am the vine; you are the branches. Whoever abides in me and I in him, he it is that bears much fruit, for apart from me you can do nothing. If anyone does not abide in me he is thrown away like a branch and withers; and the branches are gathered, thrown into the fire, and burned. If you abide in me, and my words abide in you, ask whatever you wish, and it will be done for you. By this my Father is glorified, that you bear much fruit and so prove to be my disciples. As the Father has loved me, so have I loved you. Abide in my love. If you keep my commandments, you will abide in my love, just as I have kept my Father's commandments and abide in his love. These things I have spoken to you, that my joy may be in you, and that your joy may be full.

This is my commandment, that you love one another as I have loved you. Greater love has no one than this, that someone lay down his life for his friends. You are my friends if you do what I command you. No longer do I call you servants, for the servant does not know what his master is doing; but I have called you friends, for all that I have heard from my Father I have made known to you. You did not choose me, but I chose you and appointed you that you should go and bear fruit and that your fruit should abide, so that whatever you ask the Father in my name, he may give it to you. These things I command you, so that you will love one another. John 15: 1-17

Bruce Wilkinson does an amazing job fleshing out this teaching of Jesus in his book *Secrets of the Vine*.[3] He accentuates this teaching on the pruning effects of discipline in the Christian life, which may be painful, but the purpose of pruning is to bear more fruit. We are called to

---

3. Bruce Wilkinson, *Secrets of the Vine: Breaking Through to Abundance* (Oregon: Multnomah, 2002)

abide in our relationship with the Lord, but that may mean we will have to suffer for our faith.

Theology of Risk and Suffering

With this metaphor, Jesus introduced the hard topic of risk and suffering to his followers. This was after his triumphal entry into Jerusalem but before his trial and crucifixion. John previously recorded other analogies Jesus gave like, "I am the bread of Life" and "I am the Good Shepherd," but here Jesus expanded to include his disciple's position and mission in the world by saying, "I am the Vine; you are the branches." The Holy Spirit is introduced in John chapter 14 as a "Helper," and Jesus promised not to "leave you as orphans" even though he would not be on earth with them for what is to come.

Jesus knows his followers will experience suffering and hardship just for identifying with him, so he uses this vineyard experience to explain the natural order of growth with the desired outcome of bearing fruit. This way they will know their eventual suffering is not in vain nor is it punishment for doing something wrong.

One of the most difficult truths to accept is *"every branch that does bear fruit he prunes, that it may bear more fruit."* Children do not enjoy being disciplined by their parents, but, when they are older, they tend to realize it was for their good in developing character. Similarly, believers whom the Lord disciplines need to recognize that spiritual pruning is intended to mold and shape them for his purposes.

Missionaries who are called to serve in hard-to-reach areas of the world have a very challenging task. They constantly face opposition from immigration and governmental authorities, leaders of other religions, language acquisition, cultural adaptation, education needs for their children, inadequate healthcare and more. These issues are well known by everyone in the Great Commission community—suffering is a part of the job description.

Since churches in Iran and China are growing despite persecution, we may certainly conclude that they are growing, in part, due to the pruning effects of the Vinedresser. It is a paradox and a mystery. So, what can the North American church learn from our brothers and sisters who are experiencing the pain of persecution in these far-off distant places? While we see the church growing in these places and others like them around the world, the North American church is in decline. Pew researchers state that sixty-four percent of Americans called themselves Christian in 2020, which is significantly lower than the same study in 1970 which reported ninety percent.[4] At this rate, Christians will be in the minority in North America very soon.

Rich Soil, Well-Watered, Unabated Growth

If pruning is essential for growth and health, then the church in North America would benefit from a trimming. Taking risks and submitting to the potential of suffering is counter to human nature and our incessant search for safety and security, but successful churches are not afraid of reaching out to people in places that are resistant to the gospel. Pruning away our tendencies of risk avoidance in the church is necessary for growth. Like a grapevine, the church in the New World has been planted in rich soil, it has been well watered and allowed to grow freely without any hindrance for a very long time. And yet it is declining in numbers as well as influence.

In John 15, Jesus used the vineyard as a teaching tool. Elsewhere in Scripture, wine is used to illustrate many spiritual lessons. The fermented drink was prescribed in the Old Testament for various festivals (Numbers 15:5). Wine was considered an acceptable sacrifice for the priests who worked at the Temple (Ezekiel 6:8-10). The first miracle of Jesus was turning water into wine (John 2:1-11). And at the Lord's Last Supper, wine was prescribed by Jesus for his disciples to remember his sacrifice on the cross (Matthew 26:17–30; Mark 14:12–26; Luke 22:7–39). If you think about it, both wine and bread are products that are made by human toil. Jesus did not institute just grain and grapes

---

4. "America's Christian Majority is shrinking...", McCammon, Levitt and Fox, September 15, 2022, https://www.npr.org/2022/09/15/1123289466/americas-christian-majority-is-shrinking-and-could-dip-below-50-by-2070

in their natural form for this ordinance. Bread is developed in the heat of an oven, and wine has to endure the time and process of fermentation. Both elements represent human exertion with the possibility of risk and suffering.

Since wine is frequently used for spiritual analogies in the Bible, we decided to deliberately study viniculture and the cultivation of grapes for winemaking. To do this, we began our research in a local wine cellar that belonged to our friend Faythe Laatsch-Coley. Then we decided to tour some of the vineyards of France for some contemporary insight. In this process, we discovered some remarkable insights that may help churches discover the Vinedresser's purpose as he applies the pruning shears to "the branches."

When referring to either the church or agriculture, environmental impact is important to note. Just as an environment of persecution led to the growth and expansion of the church in the first century, we are seeing that same scenario in the churches of China and Iran. But is there something more to growth than just hardship from outside influences? Can the church grow in a healthy environment by applying some agricultural principles that we glean from Scripture and in the vineyard?

Terroir

Visiting vineyards like Chateauneuf-du-Pape in France, we noticed immediately that the terrain environment (*terroir* in French) is very different than that of our corn, wheat and grain growing regions in the Midwestern United States. Most of the vineyards are on hillsides with terracing and steep slopes. The soil itself is very rocky and rugged, so the grapevine has to struggle to dig its roots down deep where the water flows.

Just as the grapevine needs to dig deep to get access to nourishing water, our churches need to dig deep by abiding in the Vine. That is the real source of all of our energy and efforts to bear fruit as believers as well as our gathered communities around the world. It isn't enough to provide surface irrigation, which only leads to shallow roots. The point of digging deeper is to strengthen the root system. When we compare the growth of the church in North America with those churches in closed countries like China and Iran, the environment is stark and vastly different.

Spiritually speaking, here in North America we have well-watered shallow roots. We have not recently had to struggle against persecution, oppression or hindrances to our gospel message. We understand that, in the end times, all believers everywhere will see this discrimination increase even here in a country founded on religious freedom. It is inevitable if you know how the story ends.

Climate

In the Bordeaux region of France, 1990 was a historically notable year for a legendary wine harvest. Pricing for that year's vintage is twice the price of other years due to the quality of the harvest. The summer months of 1990 saw record-breaking hot and dry conditions not seen since 1961 (yet another legendary vintage for that region). This set the stage for an early harvest. There were fewer grapes with smaller clusters, but they had an intensified flavor. After the crush, the concentrated fruit required more than the typical time cellaring in barrels, but the results were worth the wait. Many of these bottles are still being enjoyed more than thirty years later because of the maturity that has lingered.

One of the criticisms of mega-churches in North America is that they seem to be purposely entertaining and are watered down to attract more people. As the saying goes, "The purpose of a large church is to become a larger church." Having a sizeable crowd to reach is a good thing in some respects, but it must also be paired with a concentrated effort to grow in maturity. Most wine that is consumed in the world is mass-produced with the minimum effort necessary for production. Bloated grapes that come from well-watered vineyards are less intense, but they are more profitable. There is something special about wine that is produced during droughts and dry conditions.

We have met with several megachurch leaders and most understand this dilemma of mass-produced disciples, so they are intentionally focused on the concept of "growing smaller." They are referring to building up the maturity level of church members through small groups. Some even speak about a "church within a church," which is intended to address this concern.

In contrast, just because a church is small does not mean it is advanced in spiritual maturity. Churches, just like wine, need thoughtful and caring leaders with an emphasis on depth and complexity. It is a quality that the French refer to as *je ne sais quoi*.[5]

Pruning

The world's most expensive and collectible wine comes from the Burgundy region of France—Domaine de la Romanée-Conti (or DRC). It is a very small privately owned estate, and the average age of the vines is over fifty years; they only produce 450 cases of bottled wine per year. The average price per bottle is $21,000 (USD). The history of this vineyard is interesting since it dates back to the thirteenth century, but that is not why it is so expensive. The major reason is their cultivation practices.

Organic farming has increased in popularity around the world as producers respond to the demand for safer and healthier agriculture. When something is organic, it means there is no use of synthetic fertilizers or pesticides, but there are no restrictions on many common farming practices. Biodynamic is a step further than organic, which is what makes DRC so special. They minimize soil problems by using horse-drawn tills instead of tractors. The only fertilizer they use is crushed roots and grape skins along with fermentation residue, nothing synthetic. And the most significant part of this process is intentionally producing low yields by aggressively pruning the branches throughout the entire growing season. At the time of harvest, there is one last purge of substandard grapes, which is done individually by hand on what they call a "triage table."

---

5. "Je ne sais quoi" is a colloquial French term that is translated as "I don't know what," meaning an undefinable quality.

We asked the vinedresser about his pruning methods. His answer reminded us of John 15 and had profound implications for our understanding of the Lord's work as he prunes his church. DRC's winemaker identified the four types of branches on a grapevine: they grow toward the sky, toward the ground, out to the side and inward toward the other branches. When he is pruning, he takes away those that grow inward and downward, but he leaves and props up the ones that grow up and out.

We immediately recognized the spiritual application. Churches with an upward focus on worshipping the Lord as well as an outward focus on evangelizing are the ones that grow mature disciples. Those churches that are inward-focused and downward-oriented will eventually be taken away from the Vine. Just like the focus of this vineyard is to grow more concentrated fruit instead of a large harvest, churches that produce upward- and outward-oriented disciples will experience a better-quality harvest. Perhaps this is why Jesus spoke about the narrow gate and followed it up with a comment about bearing fruit.

Enter by the narrow gate. For the gate is wide and the way is easy that leads to destruction, and those who enter by it are many. For the gate is narrow and the way is hard that leads to life, and those who find it are few. Beware of false prophets, who come to you in sheep's clothing but inwardly are ravenous wolves. You will recognize them by their fruits. Are grapes gathered from thornbushes, or figs from thistles? So, every healthy tree bears good fruit, but the diseased tree bears bad fruit. A healthy tree cannot bear bad fruit, nor can a diseased tree bear good fruit. Every tree that does not bear good fruit is cut down and thrown into the fire. Thus, you will recognize them by their fruits.

Matthew 7:13-20

Over the last thirty years of ministry, we have enjoyed the luxury provided by a well-watered church that has grown unabated because it was planted in rich soil. But we know from our study of the vineyard that the church needs to be pruned and starved from moist, nutrient-rich soil so that our roots will grow deeper to our True Water Source. We also know from our study of eschatology (end times) that the church will eventually face seasons of dryness and oppressive heat in our emerging environment. Those days are coming, and the Lord's vineyard will need some pruning.

As we see headlines coming from places like China and Iran, we are not always sure how we can relate to them or even pray for them. Let us not be tempted to ask the Lord to remove the sufferings that our brothers and sisters are experiencing in those difficult places, but pray for them to endure. There is purpose in the suffering. But let us join with Paul as he says,

...we rejoice in our sufferings, knowing that suffering produces endurance, and endurance produces character, and character produces hope, and hope does not put us to shame, because God's love has been poured into our hearts through the Holy Spirit who has been given to us.

Romans 5:3-5

Our unconventional prayer is that the North American church will gracefully receive the eventual pruning shears of the Vinedresser with endurance, character and hope, because "...every branch in me that does bear fruit he prunes, that it may bear more fruit" (John 15:2)!

Parable of the Sower (or The Four Soils)

There are many other agricultural metaphors in Scripture that are given so we can understand the natural order of things on earth. We find it interesting that the teaching of the vineyard is only found in the Gospel of John, while the Four Soils parable is found only in the Synoptic Gospels (Matthew, Mark and Luke) but not in John. Even though they have different applications, the reason is the same. Jesus wants his followers to focus on quality instead of quantity. Bearing fruit is important, and the importance of the harvest depends not on numbers but on the quality of those who truly believe.

Jesus was known for speaking in parables, but the Parable of the Sower is the one in which he provided the reason for speaking in these mysterious ways. While many books and resources highlight the details of the four different soils in the parable, our interest for this chapter is to take a look at his reason for speaking in parables.

And when a great crowd was gathering and people from town after town came to him, he said in a parable, "A sower went out to sow his seed. And as he sowed, some fell along the path and was trampled underfoot, and the birds of the air devoured it. And some fell on the rock, and as it grew up, it withered away, because it had no moisture. And some fell among thorns, and the thorns grew up with it and choked it. And some fell into good soil and grew and yielded a hundredfold." As he said these things, he called out, "He who has ears to hear, let him hear."

And when his disciples asked him what this parable meant, he said, "To you it has been given to know the secrets of the kingdom of God, but for others they are in parables, so that 'seeing they may not see, and hearing they may not understand.' Now the parable is this: The seed is the word of God. The ones along the path are those who have heard; then the devil comes and takes away the word from their hearts, so that they may not believe and be saved. And the ones on the rock are those who, when they hear the word, receive it with joy. But these have no root; they believe for a while, and in time of testing fall away. And as for what fell among the thorns, they are those who hear, but as they go on their way they are choked by the cares and riches and pleasures of life, and their fruit does not mature. As for that in the good soil, they are those who, hearing the word, hold it fast in an honest and good heart, and bear fruit with patience.   Luke 8:4-15

If we only studied this parable by looking at the four soils described, it would be easy to conclude that we should not waste our time sharing the gospel message in places that have rocky soil or thorns (like China or Iran). But that is not the point of this parable of Jesus. This parable deals with the hearts of the individuals in the crowd and how they receive his teachings, not their circumstances. Jesus is making a distinction between true believers and those who are just going along with the crowd.

We have heard some church leaders misapply the teaching of the four soils in two different ways. First, in the aftermath of the martyrdom of missionary John Chau in 2018, a pastor in the Midwest concluded that missionaries should not be sent to hard places since the gospel will not be received by "those people." His rationale was that we should only send gospel messengers to places with "well-cultivated soil." Second, a pastor in a very poor urban area used the four soils parable to justify his church's social justice prominence and lack of emphasis on evangelism and proclamation of the gospel. His justification was that "the work of justice is removing the stones from the rocky places, and alleviating poverty is clearing out thorns so that people can see the gospel instead of hear it." Even though these ideas sound reasonable, they fall short of God's design for his church to proclaim the message of the gospel of Jesus everywhere and to everyone.

On any given weekend in religious buildings around the world, there will be true believers mingled among the crowds. People go to these gatherings for a variety of reasons: to please their friends and family, to network for business, to hear an inspirational message or because it is part of their cultural identity. For every reason under the sun, there is an organized effort to provide for their needs. But just because someone has a need does not mean they are a believer. Nor does the organized effort around that need mean that it is a church.

The word *church* on the building does not make it the branches that abide in the Lord to bear fruit for his Kingdom!

Evangelism is the work of the church and disciples are its fruit. There are so many things we see churches do in the community: food drives, blood drives, homeless and poverty alleviation, refugee resettlement, children's camps, Easter egg hunts, Christmas music recitals, funerals, weddings—the list goes on indefinitely. It can be easy to get so busy with these activities that we lose sight of *why* we are doing them. All these things are also done by civic organizations, community groups, non-profits and governmental entities. Even the traditional pastor's triad (hatch, match and dispatch) is being transitioned out of the local church. Children are christened at the hospital by chaplains. Weddings are held at wedding chapels or event venues. When was the last time you attended a funeral at a church? Funeral homes have chapels that accommodate the memorial services with far fewer complications.

So, we must ask the question, "What is the one thing the church can do that no other organization can?"

If churches stop working with homeless people, then all sorts of non-profit organizations will fill in the gap. If church leaders cease collecting food for the hungry in their city, then civic organizations like Rotary, Kiwanis and the Optimists will pick up the slack. Many non-religious camp organizations for children give kids a wilderness experience in the summer. When refugees enter the country, the government has a vast network of corporations and private entities that work together to get them resettled in an area.

Churches are very busy places with lots of activities. And in good times, when the social environment is prosperous with no obstacles to growth, church leaders do not need to reduce their activities. Sometimes these activities are like weeds, and they choke out the more important purpose of evangelism and bearing fruit. Some would never consider intentionally slowing growth unless something happens in the environment, like a terrorist attack, a pandemic or an economic collapse. We have seen churches over the years respond to these types of conditions by temporarily curtailing all the busyness of the church until they can *get back to normal*. Without fail, they always seem to work overtime just to get back to normal.

What if getting back to normal is not what the Lord wanted for the church? What if the Lord was using these events to prune the excessive growth of activities to help the church prioritize the one thing the church can do that no other organization can do? What if that crazy global pandemic we experienced recently, which necessitated the doors to our buildings be closed, was God's way of pruning the excess branches in the church? Could that have been our Vinedresser's pruning shears at work in our world? Was that a message delivered to "He who has ears to hear, let him hear?"

There is nothing wrong with these activities, as long as they are seen as a means to an end but not the end itself. A food drive to feed the hungry is a good thing. A homeless ministry is a good thing. Children's camp in the summer is a good thing. A music recital is a good thing. But Jesus did not come to earth, live a sinless life, die on the cross and rise from the dead just so we could do good things for people. The Good News has a Great Commission for the church to make disciples of all nations. Proclamation of the gospel is the work of the church, and disciples are its fruit! All other activities are a means to that end.

As an exercise, go to a quiet place and imagine you are a Christ follower in China, Iran or some other restricted access nation of the world. Legally, you are not allowed to share your faith publicly. Your family has disowned you because of your faith. There is persecution from other religions, so even your employment is limited. But you have this amazing faith that the Lord is at work in your life, and you have a profound sense that he wants you to share this with other people. What can you do?

Evangelism does not begin with the activity of sharing your faith. It begins with prayer. Through prayer, you acknowledge that you are a branch connected to the Vine, which provides you with everything you need to bear fruit. As you envision yourself being that branch and connected to the Vine, pray for your family members who do not yet know Christ. Pray for your neighbors. Pray for your coworkers. Pray for those living in other countries who are suffering persecution that they will endure in the faith with character, hope and righteousness as they grow in the Holy Spirit. When you *abide in the Vine* the Lord will use you to *bear much fruit* because *you are the branches*.

Imagine what the world would look like if every church made the Great Commission their priority, and every believer prayed for those who were lost across the street and around the world.

The Lord is building (verb) his church!
It is not a building (noun). It is a people!
A gathered and scattered people
for the sake of the gospel.

Scoring Metric for **The Branches**

This is the third in a series of exercises to help your church evaluate its practice of the seven biblical metaphors we explore in this book. Answer the questions below with a rating of 1-5. Add the results together and then divide by 5 to get the score for this chapter on evangelism and propagating the gospel. Record your results in the appendix to help you evaluate your congregation's strengths and weaknesses.

On a scale of 1-5:   Score
1. Does the church teach and practice the concept of abiding in the Lord? _____
2. Is the gospel of salvation proclaimed regularly?   _____
3. Are members taught effective personal evangelism strategies?   _____
4. Are conversions taking place?   _____
5. Are the church leaders willing to take risks for gospel propagation?   _____

                                                                Total: _____
                                                                 ÷ 5 = _____

(Record this number in the Appendix under the heading **The Branches**)

THE BRANCHES

❧ 4 ☙
THE BUILDING

This Church Sign brings clarity to the mission of the church as our identity through discipleship, accountability and discipline.

In him you also are being built together into
a dwelling place for God by the Spirit.
Ephesians 2:22

THE BUILDING

Descriptions of the Church Exemplified by the Building:

- Discipleship (9Marks, IMB Foundations)
- Accountability (IMB Foundations)
- Discipline (9Marks)

> **The Lord is building (verb) his church.**
> **It is not a building (noun). It is a people!**
> **They are a gathered and scattered**
> **people for the sake of the gospel.**

A few years after the birth of the church on the day of Pentecost in Jerusalem, a horrific persecution launched the early church toward the ends of the earth as recorded in the book of Acts. The spark that ignited the flame of this widespread persecution was a speech given to religious leaders by Stephen—"a man full of faith and of the Holy Spirit" (Acts 6:5). The first part of his message was well received since it was grounded in the history and traditions of the synagogue. Stephen displayed substantial knowledge of the Scriptures, but his audience became enraged as soon as he challenged their emphasis on the temple.

Our fathers had the tent of witness in the wilderness, just as he who spoke to Moses directed him to make it, according to the pattern that he had seen. Our fathers in turn brought it in with Joshua when they dispossessed the nations that God drove out before our fathers. So it was until the days of David, who found favor in the sight of God and asked to find a dwelling place for the God of Jacob. But it was Solomon who built a house for him. **Yet the Most High does not dwell in houses made by hands,** *as the prophet says,*

"Heaven is my throne, and the earth is my footstool.
What kind of house will you build for me,
says the Lord, or what is the place of my rest?
Did not my hand make all these things?"
You stiff-necked people, uncircumcised in heart and ears, you always

resist the Holy Spirit. As your fathers did, so do you. Which of the prophets did your fathers not persecute? And they killed those who announced beforehand the coming of the Righteous One, whom you have now betrayed and murdered, you who received the law as delivered by angels and did not keep it.

Acts 7:44-53

After this, Stephen was executed by stoning and the persecution of the church officially began. The violence recorded in Acts 8:1 led to the scattering of believers into all the world, and the Great Commission was launched just as Jesus said in Acts 1:8. The *ekklesia* became a movement of people with a powerful message, taking the temple of the Holy Spirit with them as they scattered.

Too often, the church is equated with a building—a place of worship that is comfortable and recognizable to believers. We hear our friends and family say things like, "Let's go to church," or "Turn right at the church on the corner." It is very difficult to train people to adopt the correct paradigm when buildings have signs out front labeling the place as a church.

We recently heard a pastor welcome his congregation by saying, "Good morning church, welcome to the building!" He is training his congregation to understand this biblical concept that the church is a people, not a place or an activity. He believes the church is *gathered* when they meet and *scattered* when they depart. We saw signs saying things like, "This building is where the church assembles," and "Gather to Worship, Scatter to Serve." As we were leaving, we noticed a sign in the parking lot saying, "You are now entering the mission field."

Signs are powerful! Some signs point people in a certain direction, while others reinforce appropriate thoughts or correct inappropriate behaviors. Church signs have the ability to develop a way of thinking about the church.

The speech made by Stephen regarding the Temple in Jerusalem struck at the heart of the fallacy of these religious leaders. He was not condemning their worship of God *at* the Temple; he was denouncing their worship *of* the Temple. He reminded them about their predecessors who were refusing to listen to the prophets, misapplying the Law and for all their rituals that led to idolatry. The Temple made by human hands was not the problem, but it came to symbolize the problem of an establishment that had lost its way.

Jesus also spoke hard truths against Temple leaders when he cleansed the Temple after the beginning of his earthly ministry as recorded in John 2.

The Passover of the Jews was at hand, and Jesus went up to Jerusalem. In the temple he found those who were selling oxen and sheep and pigeons, and the money-changers sitting there. And making a whip of cords, he drove them all out of the temple, with the sheep and oxen. And he poured out the coins of the money-changers and overturned their tables. And he told those who sold the pigeons, "Take these things away; do not make my Father's house a house of trade." His disciples remembered that it was written, "Zeal for your house will consume me."

So the Jews said to him, "What sign do you show us for doing these things?" Jesus answered them, "Destroy this temple, and in three days I will raise it up." The Jews then said, "It has taken forty-six years to build this temple, and will you raise it up in three days?" But he was speaking about the temple of his body. When therefore he was raised from the dead, his disciples remembered that he had said this, and they believed the Scripture and the word that Jesus had spoken.

John 2:13-22

Here, Jesus spoke metaphorically about his bodily resurrection and introduced his followers to the concept of a temple that is not made with human hands. Jesus knew the religious leaders of the Temple in Jerusalem would reject the Messiah because it had been prophesied in Psalm 118. Jesus quoted this forewarning in Matthew 21 the week before His crucifixion.

The stone that the builders rejected has become the cornerstone.
This is the LORD's doing; it is marvelous in our eyes.

Psalm 118:22-23

Jesus said to them, "Have you never read in the Scriptures:
'The stone that the builders rejected has become the cornerstone;
this was the Lord's doing, and it is marvelous in our eyes'?
Therefore I tell you, the kingdom of God will be taken away from you
and given to a people producing its fruits. And the one who falls on this
stone will be broken to pieces; and when it falls on anyone, it will crush
him." When the chief priests and the Pharisees heard his parables, they
perceived that he was speaking about them.

Matthew 21:42-45

Idolatry of Place

The *idolatry of place* is a frequent subject throughout the Old Testament. The people of God have always been called and set apart to be holy. The word *holy* (*qadosh* in Hebrew) means "separated to live according to the purposes of God." In the context of the Israelites, God called them to not be like their neighbors who set up "high places" for the worship of their pagan gods like Baal. The idolatry represented by these high places prevented people from having an intimate relationship with the Almighty Creator God of Israel.

Idolatry is just as real today as it was thousands of years ago; it just takes on a different form. Whatever replaces God as a priority in your life is an idol. It could be a job, family or friends, luxuries or even religion. All of these things are good when aptly prioritized with the Lord at the center of them all. Even a church building can become an unhealthy obsession as it did for the religious leaders in Jesus' day. When the institution and all that encompasses it begins to take priority, leaders need to recognize it as idolatry and repent and reprioritize.

The religious leaders at the Temple in Jerusalem were political leaders as well. It was not just the building they were protecting but the institution that gave them their status. Their livelihood was under attack by John the Baptist, Jesus and this burgeoning movement of the Holy Spirit in Christ-followers. They prioritized their status and occupation over and above what the Lord was doing in their midst.

When the Israelites entered the Promised Land, they were instructed to destroy all the high places on which the pagans had erected shrines and altars. They built these structures on mountain tops and elevated places under the assumption that they could be nearer to their gods. Time and time again we read in the Old Testament the ominous words, "Nevertheless, the high places were not removed" (2 Kings 12:3, 14:4, 15:4, 15:35). Kings, judges and other leaders refused to take the Lord's words seriously, and the people paid a heavy price for their disobedience. King Josiah was one of the few agents of God who fulfilled the Word of the Lord by removing the high places. He is known as the king who would obey God by doing the hard work no matter how popular or conventional the idolatry had become (2 Kings 23).

God in a Box

One of the unfortunate side effects of having church buildings is that people see themselves as drawing near to God when they come to the building but not very close to Him when at home, at work or in their neighborhood. It takes intentionality on the part of the believer to draw close to the Lord outside of the building. Church leaders must be proactive in helping the saints see themselves as the church in all of their places of influence. Made to Flourish[1] is an organization started by Pastor Tom Nelson, author of *Work Matters: Connecting Sunday Worship to Monday Work*.[2] They provide excellent resources to help churches and pastors enlarge their circles of influence beyond the walls of the building.

As humans, we like to understand things. It is comfortable when we organize our thoughts and compartmentalize the world that surrounds us. When we are hungry, we go to restaurants, eat-in dining rooms or open the refrigerator. These are all boxes in a metaphorical sense. When we want information, we have the television, radio, the computer or our handheld devices. Again, these are boxes. For education, we have the

---

1. Made to Flourish, https://www.madetoflourish.org/about continuously updated. (Accessed March 25, 2024)
2. Tom Nelson, "Work Matters: Connecting Sunday Worship to Monday Work" (Wheaton: Crossway, 2021)

schoolhouse. For entertainment, we have movie theaters. For healthcare, we have hospitals and urgent care clinics—affectionately known as "Doc in a Box." So, it is consistent that we would put *God in a Box* for our spiritual needs in a church building. But that goes against the Lord's command for his people to be holy and set apart for a higher purpose in all areas of our lives.

We love to travel to Europe and tour the grand cathedrals that are scattered across the continent. When we enter the massive doorways, our eyes are immediately drawn upward to view the majestic architecture of the soaring vaulted ceilings. Cathedral designs are intended to evoke emotion at the grandeur and splendor so that we will raise our eyes toward heaven and away from the world. Many of these buildings took hundreds of years to complete, which means the architect and those who laid the cornerstone at the beginning of construction knew they would never be able to participate in the completion of the church. If the church were defined as a building, these people, and many generations after them, would never know the joy of being the church. They were merely church builders. But Jesus is the church builder! He said he would build his church, (Matthew 16:18), so he obviously was talking about something very different than cathedrals, chapels, shrines, sanctuaries or tabernacles.

Many of these cathedrals in Europe have been transformed for other purposes like mosques, shrines, tourist attractions, museums, music halls and other secular uses. Think of all the energy and expense that was used to erect these massive buildings that were meant to stand the test of time, only to be converted into a "place of interest." If only church leaders at the time had a proper understanding of the church that Jesus was building, all of that time, energy and money could have been used for gospel expansion rather than a monument for a dying institution.

When we put God in the box of a building, we are instituting limits on him and his people. We need a movement of God's people to be unleashed in our neighborhoods and among the nations! When believers are equipped with the knowledge that God can use them anywhere and everywhere, the world will take notice. Unfortunately, these ideas have a way of challenging the theological boxes that have become so important to our congregations. Thankfully, God cannot be contained in these boxes, but like Stephen, those who speak out of the box are often persecuted by those within the box.

Saul Heard Stephen's Speech

The Apostle Paul (formerly known as Saul) was present when Stephen said the words, "Yet the Most High does not dwell in houses made by human hands" (Acts 7:48). He was there to give approval for the execution. Scripture tells us that Saul ravaged the church by dragging believers out of their homes and putting them in prison. Soon, thereafter, he had his moment of conversion with the risen Christ who asked, "Saul, why are you persecuting me?... I am Jesus, whom you are persecuting" (Acts 9:4-5).

In this passage. Jesus was expressing one of the most intimate examples of a relationship with his church—his Bride. Notice how he doesn't say, "You are persecuting my people." Rather, Jesus was equating himself with his followers who were experiencing this persecution—not a building being torn down or an institution being threatened but a people who personally identify with their God. Perhaps this is what Paul was thinking about when he said to the Corinthian church, "Do you not know that you [plural] are God's temple and that God's Spirit dwells in you? If anyone destroys God's temple, God will destroy him. For God's temple is holy, and you are that temple" (1 Corinthians 3:16-17). He also echoed this emphasis of the new temple of the Lord in his letter to the Ephesians.

So then you are no longer strangers and aliens, but you are fellow citizens with the saints and members of the household of God, built on the foundation of the apostles and prophets, Christ Jesus himself being the cornerstone, in whom the whole structure, being joined together, grows into a holy temple in the Lord. In him you also are being built together into a dwelling place for God by the Spirit.

Ephesians 2:19-22

If we collectively are the temple and dwelling place of the Holy Spirit, then we need to formulate a more robust way of describing the ekklesia (the assembled church) based on the mystery and paradox found in the other metaphors we are exploring in this book. Paul described the church as a "household of God" (family). If someone were to ask you to describe your family, you would never begin by saying, "My family is located on the corner of 5th and Vine. We meet there every Saturday for brunch at 11 a.m. We usually have two meats, and three side dishes and the kids eat at a separate table. There are fifteen of us when everyone shows up for the family meal." In this example, the family is described by its location and activity and not by its identity and relationship. We so often describe the church either by place or activity. But the church is our identity as a people of Almighty God. It cannot be reduced to a place or an action.

The word *church* on the building does not make it the church that Jesus is building!

The true sign of the church is found as a gathered and scattered people who are indwelled by the Holy Spirit all week long in every place, in every relationship and in every activity. Paul was impacted by Stephen's message about a building not made by human hands. He referenced this in other letters like 1 Corinthians where he takes the temple concept one step further and applies it to people.

Flee from sexual immorality. Every other sin a person commits is outside the body, but the sexually immoral person sins against his own body. Or do you not know that your body is a temple of the Holy Spirit within you, whom you have from God? You are not your own, for you were bought with a price. So glorify God in your body.

1 Corinthians 6:18-20

Personal responsibility and accountability were primary concerns for both apostles, Paul and Peter, as they wrote letters to the early church. In times before Christ, the Temple was the place of sacrifices that were prescribed and conducted by the religious leaders of the community. But thanks to Christ's final and definitive sacrifice on the cross as the Lamb of God, propitiation for sin has been accomplished once and for all. We are held accountable by each other based on our relationship to Him.

As you come to him, a living stone rejected by men but in the sight of God chosen and precious, you yourselves like living stones are being built up as a spiritual house, to be a holy priesthood, to offer spiritual sacrifices acceptable to God through Jesus Christ. For it stands in Scripture: "Behold, I am laying in Zion a stone, a cornerstone chosen and precious," and "whoever believes in him will not be put to shame."

So the honor is for you who believe, but for those who do not believe, "The stone that the builders rejected has become the cornerstone," *and* "A stone of stumbling, and a rock of offense." *They stumble because they disobey the word, as they were destined to do.*

But you are a chosen race, a royal priesthood, a holy nation, a people for his own possession, that you may proclaim the excellencies of him who called you out of darkness into his marvelous light. Once you were not a people, but now you are God's people; once you had not received mercy, but now you have received mercy.

1 Peter 2:4-10

Discipleship

Discipleship is not a word that is used in the Bible. The Lord Jesus commissioned his church to go into all the world and make disciples, but even the word *disciple* fell out of use after the historical accounts in the New Testament. Acts 21:16 is the last time that word is used. The epistles were letters written by Paul, Peter and others for instruction to the church, and yet none of them explain what a disciple is or even list the qualities found in a disciple. The English word disciple comes to us from the Latin word *discipulus*, which was the translation of the Greek word *mathetes*. Some may simplify the significance of the word by saying it means "a learner," but that only undermines the efforts of biblical scholars who preserved the word and sought to convey something more profound.

In ancient times, people who were experts in a trade would engage apprentices to work alongside and learn the skills of the master craftsman. They were more than just students involved in learning. They were fully engaged in the work of that trade. In like manner of an apprenticeship, teachers and philosophers would take disciples to learn and practice their craft. They were more than just a pupil, student or even a scholar. The disciple was a devotee to the religion or philosophy while being actively engaged as a trainee.

Many churches struggle with the concept of discipleship, so perhaps a more biblical concept is disciple-making. Too often, it is just a Bible study or an activity within the walls of the building. Disciples in the local church today are often invited to discipleship training, but when it comes time to go out and practice what they learned, they are rarely accompanied by the teacher. One of the key components of disciple-making is the master-apprentice relationship. Disciples need to see the work in action so they learn to emulate one who has mastered the skills.

Disciple-making in the church is more than just externally learning a skill or practicing the faith. There needs to be work on the inmost being of the believer as well. The heart of a disciple was a chief concern of Jesus, and the formation of the spirit has emerged as a pervasive need in the church. Dallas Willard uses the term "spiritual formation" and describes it as a "formation of the inner being of the human being, resulting in the transformation of the whole person, including the body in its social context."[3] Willard describes this formation as an internal process with an external result. He also distinguishes the difference between being a Christian and being a disciple.

> Spiritual formation could and should be the process by which those who are Jesus' apprentices or disciples come easily to "do all things whatsoever I have commanded you." What I call "the great omission from the great commission" is the fact that Christians generally don't have a plan for teaching people to do everything that he commanded. We

---

3. Dallas Willard, "Spiritual Formation: What it is, and How it is Done", https://dwillard.org/resources/articles/spiritual-formation-what-it-is-and-how-it-is-done (March 30, 2024)

don't as a rule even have a plan for learning this ourselves, and perhaps assume it is simply impossible. And that explains the yawning abyss today between being Christian and being a disciple. We have a form of religion that has accepted non-obedience to Christ, and the hunger for spirituality and spiritual formation in our day is a direct consequence of that.[4]

Just as having a building was not part of the original biblical design of the church, establishing a discipleship program was not either. Compare the model of Jesus with the model of the religious leaders of his day. You cannot program the Holy Spirit's work on the innermost parts of a believer. This metaphor of *being* the temple of the Holy Spirit must be more intentional and proactive than simply exploring your faith, attending a class, taking five easy steps, and all the other programs we see in churches. Making disciples requires accountability, discipline and difficult decisions that are very unpopular. Steven was martyred because he sought to hold those religious leaders accountable for their hypocrisy and distortion of the Temple. This is why churches struggle with discipleship—it takes too much work. The easy way is to manage the institution.

Accountability and Discipline

Peter was present for the only two instances when Jesus used the word church (ekklesia) during his earthly ministry (Matthew 16:16-20, 18:15-20). On both occasions, Jesus used the words *bind* (*deses*) and *loose* (*lyses*), which means "to prohibit and to permit." These two Greek words are most often used in the context of a prison, as in prison doors being locked or opened, or a prisoner in chains and shackles being constrained or freed. Pay attention to the way Jesus described his vision for the church in this passage from the Gospel of Matthew.

---

4. Ibid.

If your brother sins against you, go and tell him his fault, between you and him alone. If he listens to you, you have gained your brother. But if he does not listen, take one or two others along with you, that every charge may be established by the evidence of two or three witnesses. If he refuses to listen to them, tell it to the church. And if he refuses to listen even to the church, let him be to you as a Gentile and a tax collector. Truly, I say to you, whatever you bind on earth shall be bound in heaven, and whatever you loose on earth shall be loosed in heaven. Again I say to you, if two of you agree on earth about anything they ask, it will be done for them by my Father in heaven. For where two or three are gathered in my name, there am I among them.

Matthew 18:15-20

The context of this passage in Matthew is church discipline and how to hold one another accountable for our actions. Since the temple of the Holy Spirit is within us, and part of temple work is sacrificial, we are responsible and accountable to each other in Christ. There are four layers of accountability in this passage. The first layer is the *individual reconciliation*. When there is a disagreement between two believers, they are to do everything to resolve the problem among themselves in private to reestablish their relationship in Christ. The second layer is *objective intercession*. It is prescribed for those instances when two people are unable to resolve the problem on their own. Sometimes, when problems are too intense and personal, it is helpful to have two or three people who can bring an impartial, detached or unbiased perspective to the conflict. This level of problem-solving also has the purpose of restoration and reconciliation.

The third layer is *mediation*. The church (an assembly of believers) is herein charged with a very important role to stand in the gap between heaven and earth with the keys given by Christ. When a conflict rises to this level, chances of reconciliation are rare, so the purpose becomes the resolution of the problem. There is still hope of restoration, but that will depend on the maturity of the two parties involved. This layer of mediating a conflict should be taken with utmost solemnity because the results are eternal as we will see in the fourth layer which is *litigation*.

Litigation, commonly known as *church discipline* but also referred to as *excommunication* in some circles, carries with it some legal overtones since a sentence is passed and a disassociation takes place. A person or a group may be removed from participation in community life. This is a difficult concept for those of us in the twenty-first century. The practice of church discipline made sense in a closed and remote community, but when there are multiple fellowships within a thirty-minute drive, like in North America, people can just move to another assembly in town. That happens all the time because conflict avoidance is the unhealthy fruit of institutions that lose their vision.

There are denominations and other Christian organizations that are notoriously passive, seeking to avoid conflict at all costs. In their efforts to avoid conflict, they regularly have new church planting efforts by people who could not resolve interpersonal issues in their previous church. This is obvious when there are scores of small buildings with a sign that says "church" on the outside, but on the inside are just a handful of people who are not very interested in welcoming outsiders. The more people who attend, the greater the chances there will be conflict. And conflict must be avoided by these people with little to no regard for seeking a redemptive relationship with a broader church community. Conflicts will happen, so the Lord gave us a process to handle all of the issues that will eventually appear within the church. The absence of conflict is not the goal, but mature believers will see redemption as they work through the process that Jesus prescribed.

Discipline, conflict resolution skills and accountability all seem to be downers; but in reality, they are necessary for a functioning church movement. It takes sacrificial work to build the type of spiritual house Peter described, "You yourselves like living stones are being built up as a spiritual house, to be a holy priesthood, to offer spiritual sacrifices acceptable to God through Jesus Christ" (1 Peter 2:5).

Syncretism

Syncretism is a term used to describe the unhealthy fusion of different forms of beliefs and practices like what we find in 2 Kings 17:24-41. It can lead to sinful compromises, including a lack of accountability and discipline, which often results in divisions and fragmentation of the church body. We were able to visit Mozambique in the late 1990s after a brutal civil war. Communism had dominated the nation for nearly forty years, and the church struggled because it had been cut off from the broader Christian community. We saw remnants of the church that survived, but the people were very weary. Buildings that once served as meeting places for many different denominations were left in disarray. Some of them had sacrificial alters and relics of ancestral worship. There was a mix of Christianity and paganism—what missiologists would label as *syncretism*.

During that time, Mozambique was isolated from outsiders—the church lost its vision and identity. They began compromising their faith and allowing local customs to influence their practices. Church leaders were overwhelmed because they did not have support from churches in other places around the world. This example on a macro level can also happen on a micro level in individuals as well.

Churches, mission agencies and seminaries all need each other for accountability and vigorous discipline. The human condition always takes the path of least resistance. Without that support in Mozambique, church leaders began to allow one unhealthy practice after the other. It didn't happen all at once; it took forty years of seclusion before they realized they had compromised the gospel and taken the nonresistant path of syncretism.

Compromise leads to many problems within the church; but equally so, rigidity hinders the advancement of the gospel outside of the church. Both paths contain a stone of stumbling. The solution is to have a healthy tension between being interconnected with other likeminded believers while remaining interdependent. Unfortunately, many church leaders are so busy building their own siloed kingdoms of a "boxed-in god" that it is rare to find harmony between churches. That is primarily because they keep seeking *uniformity* instead of the biblical concept of *unity* (Ephesians 4:13; 1 Peter 3:8).

Some denominations and church networks practice what is commonly known as autonomy. Different churches choose to relate to each other by contributing to a common cause like missions, disaster relief, poverty alleviation and many others. They may not agree with each other in some matters of doctrine or practice, but they can align under the shared purpose of helping others. This keeps them connected while maintaining their own unique identity.

Similarly, seminaries, churches, mission agencies and others come together regularly at conferences and regional events to discuss current events and common problems. They learn from each other and share solutions to these difficult issues as a way of being interdependent.

Being interconnected as well as interdependent allows the church the flexibility to grow as well as remain true to the calling of the Lord globally and locally. This is true of organizations just as it is true of individuals. Holding each other accountable, providing discipline, and growing as disciples are the outcomes of a healthy church. Syncretism in the North American church makes it look like just another business or secular organization. With a focus on buildings, assets, personnel and outcomes orientation, the church is just another good deeds organization with a non-profit label.

For many church leaders, having a bigger building is *the* sign of a healthy church. Increasing seating capacity is considered the goal rather than a means to an end. The focus can become "more and more" rather than "healthier and healthier." The church that Jesus is building is not a place but a people who are gathered and scattered for the sake of the gospel. Those buildings we see all over town with steeples and signs out front may not be churches. They may be meeting places for the church, but, just like the cathedrals in Europe or the Temple in Jerusalem, they have the potential of becoming "like whitewashed tombs, which outwardly appear beautiful, but within are full of dead people's bones and all uncleanness" (Matthew 23:27).

The church of the living God is not made by human hands; it is a gathering of people who are being built up into a living temple where they live sacrificially for a kingdom that is not of this world. We may have buildings, but those are only tools for the church to use. Sometimes that tool is useful, but at other times the tool is a hindrance. We all need the reminder that "the Most High does not dwell in houses made by hands," or we may receive the condemnation that Stephen gave to the religious leaders of his day. "You stiff-necked people, uncircumcised in heart and ears, you always resist the Holy Spirit" (Acts 7:51). Church leaders, mission agencies and seminaries all need to be interconnected and interdependent so that all will "maintain the unity of the Spirit in the bond of peace" (Ephesians 4:3).

> **The Lord is building (verb) his church.**
> **It is not a building (noun). It is a people!**
> **They are a gathered and scattered**
> **people for the sake of the gospel.**

THE BUILDING

Scoring Metric for **The Building**

This is the fourth in a series of exercises to help your church evaluate its practice of the seven biblical metaphors we explore in this book. Answer the questions below with a rating of 1-5. Add the results together and then divide by 5 to get the score for this chapter on discipleship, accountability and discipline.

On a scale of 1-5:   Score

1. Is the building seen as a tool to be used by the people who are the church? _____
2. Is discipleship regularly taught and practiced? _____
3. Is anyone in leadership assigned the task of conflict resolution? _____
4. How strong is the interconnection with other churches and organizations? _____
5. Is there an interdependent relationship with any outside groups? _____

Total: _____

÷ 5 = _____

(Record this number in the Appendix under the heading **The Building**)

5
THE BROTHERS AND SISTERS

This church sign brings clarity to the church's mission
of fellowship between members of God's family.

*For whoever does the will of my Father in heaven
is my brother and sister and mother.*
Matthew 12:50

Descriptions of the Church Exemplified by Brothers and Sisters:

- Membership (IMB Foundations, 9Marks)
- Fellowship (Purpose Driven Church, IMB Foundations)

The church that personifies the family of God is both refreshing and daunting for many of us who come from dysfunctional earthly families. At the outset of this chapter, we must acknowledge that this may be a difficult biblical metaphor for those who have had a less-than-positive family experience. Perhaps you are part of the thirty percent of our nation who grew up without both parents in the home. According to the U.S. census data in 1968, eighty-five percent of children under eighteen lived with two parents; by 2020, seventy percent did. So, in fifty years, the percentage of children raised in single-parent families doubled, and there is no sign that it will improve.[1] A researcher at Cornell University, Karl Pillemer, writes in his book *Fault Lines: Fractured Families and How to Mend Them* that at any given time, twenty-seven percent of Americans are alienated from members of their nuclear family. If you are among those who are estranged from brothers, sisters, mother, father, spouse or children, you may find this difficult reading.

In a similar vein, many of you have had a less-than-positive church experience in the past, which can also affect your eagerness to be vulnerable enough to join a church seeking to be as intimate as a family. We meet former pastors all the time who were either removed, forced out or burned out from their positions. Sometimes this has been justifiable because of sin or error, but most premature departures are because the leader was a wrong fit. The institution needed a different style, personality or acumen. When thinking about the metaphor of a church that is a "family of God," the idea of having someone who is a wrong fit is not something that happens in a healthy family. We don't change out family members because we disagree. Marriage and family therapists work tirelessly to keep families intact, even in the midst of challenging interpersonal family relationships. Some of those same counseling techniques are frequently deployed by church consultants to help heal divisions within congregations before it's too late.

---

1. United States Census Bureau, www.census.gov (accessed May 30, 2023).

The word *church* on the building does not make it the family of God.

We interviewed people who were looking for something specific in a church home. They were looking for a place where they fit, such as a fellowship of likeminded believers with the same priorities, life experience and worldviews. While all that is good, it is also something that does not happen in a family! "You can choose your friends, but you can't choose your family," as the old saying goes. The church is not intended to be an echo chamber with everyone in full agreement on every aspect of theology. Neither is a family. That would be uniformity. You will see in some of Paul's letters to his burgeoning church that he is calling for unity, which is far more biblical than uniformity.

It is absolutely critical that you find agreement within the church family on the important fundamentals of our faith, but it is equally critical that you extend grace on secondary issues. A popular mantra among many Protestants is often attributed to St. Augustine, "In essentials unity, in non-essentials liberty, in all things charity (or love)." That sounds like good advice for both our earthly families as well as our spiritual families in the local church.

This concept of a church family is a mystery and a paradox that leaves us with a conundrum. How are we to be a family of God when any given church is constituted and organized to be an institution with many needs like children's ministry volunteers, worship musicians, staffing, mission statements and other elements that resemble something more like a business? And how are we to understand the concept of family when our earthly families are imperfect, often dysfunctional, and by all measures, becoming increasingly broken?

As we investigate this family metaphor of the church, it is important that we reverse engineer the "church as family" concept. We are not looking for the church to reflect how we see the family in its current state. Nor should we look to our earthly siblings as examples to find our spiritual family in the church. And we especially want to avoid seeing God through the lens of our relationships with our earthly parents. Rather, we want to see things from a heavenly perspective; a perfect heavenly Father who has gifted us with an ideal for his church that we can decipher through an intimate family metaphor, which we can emulate in our lives. The local church can be a family, not like our imperfect ones of this world, but we see the out-of-this-world kind of family in the Gospel of Matthew.

While he [Jesus] was still speaking to the people, behold, his mother and his brothers stood outside, asking to speak to him. But he replied to the man who told him, "Who is my mother, and who are my brothers?" And stretching out his hand toward his disciples, he said, "Here are my mother and my brothers! For whoever does the will of my Father in heaven is my brother and sister and mother."

Matthew 12:46-50

In this passage, Jesus makes it clear that his priority is for those who are spiritual brothers and sisters above that of his blood family members. As we seek to emulate the thoughts and actions of Christ, it is helpful to remember that even Jesus set his priorities on the kingdom of God above and beyond his temporal earthly family. You may come from a healthy background and have wonderful supportive people in your family. Is it possible to place too high of a priority on your earthly family? Consider these terms: helicopter parenting, nepotism and sibling favoritism. The possibility exists for idolatry when someone puts anything, including family, ahead of the priorities of God.

There is no evidence to suggest that Jesus abandoned his earthly family, nor is there evidence that his family was in disobedience to our heavenly Father. This story should not be used as justification to disrespect your earthly family. Jesus simply took a timely moment to lift his audience to a place of deep regard and demonstrate the significance of his followers as he was building his church.

In the Wilson household, we have learned how to devote ourselves to the Lord as well as to each other with some semblance of harmony. As we have served in a church, we have noticed a delicate balance between meeting the needs of the congregation as well as the needs of the home. When talking about priorities, nonbelievers often think in terms of a linear approach, like saying, "We will make something our priority, but that means another thing will be our second priority." Something very important will have to take second place or third place and then there will also be something that has to take last place in your lives. From our experience, we don't make a list of priorities like this:

1. God
2. Family
3. Work
4. Other

Instead, we make God our only priority, and that becomes a reflection of all of our other relationships. Our priority for the Lord colors all of our other relationships. Instead of the linear approach, think of it like a list of ingredients in a cake for a child. All the ingredients are important (flour, sugar, baking powder, vanilla, pineapple, etc.), but when you add the blue food dye into the mix, it is immediately transformed. The cake will taste the same, but your six-year-old may even squeal with delight when you cut into it. God takes our ordinary relationships and makes them extraordinary.

In his Sermon on the Mount, Jesus addressed the crowd to help them reprioritize their lives around being focused on God's family. He recognized that people are prone to worry about simple things like food, clothing and housing. His assurances are just as relevant today as when he said,

Therefore do not be anxious, saying, "What shall we eat?" or "What shall we drink?" or "What shall we wear?" For the Gentiles seek after all these things, and your heavenly Father knows that you need them all. But seek first the kingdom of God and his righteousness, and all these things will be added to you.

Matthew 6:31-33

Here, Jesus is saying to the crowd that they have a generous and faithful Father in heaven who will provide for their every need when they put their trust in him completely. All the other priorities in life will be handled when our heavenly Father is given his rightful place as head of the family.

Brothers and Sisters

The emerging and frequent scriptural use of the words *brother* and *sister* (*adelphos* kai *adelphe*) appears to be the most popular way those in the first-century church referred to each other in their assemblies.

As we look through the New Testament, we discover that the word *disciple* disappears after Luke's historical accounts of the church in the book of Acts, not to be seen again in any of the Epistles or the book of Revelation. Those twelve disciples in the gospels are given the title and responsibility of "Apostles" (or sent ones) in Acts and through the rest of the New Testament as they were sent out and assumed leadership of the early church. Additionally, the word *Christian* was mostly used in a derogatory sense, mainly by outsiders during the early church era. New Testament writers frequently used the familial terms brothers and sisters. We can find other terms like *saints*, *friends*, *followers*, and *servants*, but the familial terms far outnumber any others.

Counter-Cultural

We know the first century in this middle eastern region of the world where the church began was a male-dominated society. Therefore, when we read the Scriptures, we need to understand that it was perfectly acceptable linguistically to use the masculine plural form of the noun to describe an inclusive and mixed-gender gathering as brothers. However, it is interesting to notice in this passage of Matthew 12 that Jesus uses the feminine word *sisters* also. Jesus went out of the way of conventional norms to elevate the status of the women who were following him, listening to his teaching and serving in leadership roles. Having brothers *and* sisters was obviously important to Him. Time and again we read in Scripture where Jesus elevated the status of women above the cultural standards of his day, such as Mary, Martha, the woman at the well, the woman caught in adultery and others. He valued every member of his new family just like a healthy family that fully values each other.

Similarly, the Apostle Paul, in his letter to the Philippians, addressed the mixed-gender gathered church family by using the plural word for brothers (*adelphoi*). It is evident that he is speaking to both men and women since he names two of the women who were in leadership in the next sentence.

Therefore, my brothers, whom I love and long for, my joy and crown, stand firm thus in the Lord, my beloved. I entreat Euodia and I entreat Syntyche to agree in the Lord. Yes, I ask you also, true companion, help these women, who have labored side by side with me in the gospel together with Clement and the rest of my fellow workers, whose names are in the book of life.

Philippians 4:1-3

For the Apostle Paul to recognize two women in a church who "labored side by side with [him]" speaks to his ideal of unity of service for the sake of the gospel. Even though they had different roles and functions, both men and women were equal participants in service to our Father. For a male-dominated society in the first century, these were radical ideas and concepts. Even though this seems unimpressive to the modern reader, this sentence demonstrates Paul's experience of engaging women in ministry beyond the culturally accepted norms of the time.

Both Jesus and Paul used family language to convey a sense of togetherness and unity of vision and direction for this movement they started. These individual followers came together and formed spiritual families so they could endure the hardships that were about to come their way. The Roman and Jewish societies were openly hostile to this burgeoning group, so they had to band together as a family—men and women, leaders and followers, rich and poor alike. They formed a household of God (*oikos tou Theou* in Greek) that would stand against persecution. Paul wrote to Timothy.

I hope to come to you soon, but I am writing these things to you so that, if I delay, you may know how one ought to behave in the **household of God**, *which is the church of the living God, a pillar and buttress of the truth.*

1 Timothy 3:14-15

Household of God

Paul indeed equates the household of God with the church (ekklesia) in another familial term—*oikos*. Oikos means family, lineage or descendants. This was also radical because the Jewish faith taught that they alone were the children of God and that his dwelling place was the Temple in Jerusalem.

The first time we see the house of God imagery is with one of the patriarchs: Jacob's dream of the ladder to heaven. *Bethel* is the Hebrew word for house (*beth*) of God (*El*, a shortened form of *Elohim*). In his dream, Jacob says, "How awesome is this place! This is none other than the house of God, and this is the gate of heaven" (Genesis 28:17). In this passage, the focus is on a place—or house—for God, not necessarily a family dwelling like that of a household for believers. Additionally, the tabernacle was a place where the children of Israel went to worship the Lord. "And let them make me a sanctuary, that I may dwell in their midst" (Exodus 25:8). Notice the distance of this relationship as compared to the closeness we see of the church being the household of God, where God is our Father and we are his children. "But to all who did receive him, who believed in his name, he gave the right to become children of God" (John 1:12).

As believers in Jesus Christ, we are not just children of a nation-state like Israel; we have a direct link to our heavenly Father through our adoption into his family. As believers, we also have been born again into the family of God. These two concepts (adoption and birthright) were written for two different audiences, but, combined, they give us a deep and abiding picture of how we are to understand the Lord's perspective of our spiritual family.

For those in the New Testament era, there are two distinct audiences —members of the Roman culture and those of the Jewish culture. So, our biblical writers were faced with the challenge of explaining the mystery and the paradox of God's family from two different perspectives —adoption and birthright (born again).

Adoption

Paul uses the analogy of adoption frequently in his letters to the churches in the Gentile world (Galatians 4:5; Romans 8:15; Ephesians 1:5). It is true to his theological understanding as a Jewish scholar even prior to his conversion and acceptance of Christ as the messianic promise. Adoption was a common practice in the Roman world, so it would have been a familiar concept for Gentiles. The practice was often used by prominent citizens as a means to transfer wealth and property to the next generation, such as was depicted in the 1959 epic film *Ben-Hur*. Men of enormous wealth would form a legal agreement to adopt someone (even as an adult) who would take over the business, farm or property in the absence of a clear heir to the inheritance.

There are a couple of interesting side notes regarding adoption in the Roman world and how it intersects with our biblical idea of adoption into the family of God. First, this practice of adopting an heir was not just in the case of the absence of a first-born male child. Sometimes the father would deem the son as either incapable or even unworthy to manage his assets after his death. Therefore, the adopted son would fulfill the obligations of the father and replace the first-born son.

Second, adoption in the first century was considered irreversible. Once the legal adoption was approved, the adoptee would receive a new name, and he would have all the rights and benefits of the first-born son, plus the additional benefit of permanence. A father could legally disown his biological heir but not his adopted son. Paul highlights the law and adoption in his letter to the Galatians.

But when the fullness of time had come, God sent forth his Son, born of woman, born under the law, to redeem those who were under the law, so that we might receive adoptions as sons. And because you are sons, God has sent the Spirit of his Son into our hearts, crying, "Abba! Father!" So you are no longer a slave, but a son, and if a son, then an heir through God.   Galatians 4:4-7

Birthright (Born Again)

Adoption was not as common in the Jewish world as it was among the Gentiles. One's position in an Israelite community was determined based on birthright. You can get a glimpse of this phenomenon of Israelite society by reading the Old Testament book of Ruth. In the story, we see that Ruth's first husband died and left her childless. She began the search for a kinsman redeemer, a member of her late husband's family, who would provide her with a son. And when that son was born, he would be considered the son of the dead husband to carry on the family name and inheritance.

With this cultural backdrop, the Gospel of John recorded a meeting between Jesus and Nicodemus, a religious leader, when he explained that we must be born again (or born from above) into a spiritual family of God.

Now there was a man of the Pharisees named Nicodemus, a ruler of the Jews. This man came to Jesus by night and said to him, "Rabbi, we know that you are a teacher come from God, for no one can do these signs that you do unless God is with him." Jesus answered him, "Truly, truly, I say to you unless one is born again he cannot see the kingdom of God." Nicodemus said to him, "How can a man be born when he is old? Can he enter a second time into his mother's womb and be born?" Jesus answered, "Truly, truly, I say to you, unless one is born of water and the Spirit, he cannot enter the kingdom of God. That which is born of the flesh is flesh, and that which is born of Sprit is spirit."

John 3:1-6

Jesus is speaking to a Jewish leader using Jewish concepts to convey the idea of being reborn into the family of God. Using both analogies of adoption, as well as birthright, our New Testament writers address two different perspectives, but both end up with the same result—the inheritance of the kingdom as children of God.

Inheritance

The Gospel according to John states, "... to all who did receive him, who believed in his name, he gave the right to become children of God, who were born, not of blood nor the will of the flesh nor the will of man, but of God" (John 1:12-13).

In these verses, we see that we have the right to join God's family as his children *by believing in the name of Jesus*. This right was passed down to us not because of bloodline or anything that could derive from our temporal world, but solely based upon God's will through *belief in the name of Jesus*. And with that right, we have blessings as well as accountability.

.... In love he predestined us for adoption to himself as sons through Jesus Christ, according to the purpose of his will, to the praise of his glorious grace, with which he has blessed us in the Beloved. In him we have redemption through his blood, the forgiveness of our trespasses, according to the riches of his grace, which he lavished upon us, in all wisdom and insight making known to us the mystery of his will, according to his purpose, which he set forth in Christ as a plan for the fullness of time, to unite all things in him, things in heaven and things on earth.

In him we have obtained an inheritance, having been predestined according to the purpose of him who works all things according to the counsel of his will, so that we who were the first to hope in Christ might be to the praise of his glory. In him you also, when you heard the word of truth, the gospel of your salvation, and believed in him, were sealed with the promised Holy Spirit, who is the guarantee of our inheritance until we acquire possession of it, to the praise of his glory.

Ephesians 1:4-14

There are rights as well as responsibilities for members of every family, even in the church. Our heavenly Father trains us to form new ways of relating to family members. Sometimes, this training can be painful, so the Bible uses the word *discipline* to describe that training.

My son, do not regard lightly the discipline of the Lord, nor be weary when reproved by him. For the Lord disciplines the one he loves and chastises every son whom he receives. It is for discipline that you have to endure. God is treating you as sons. For what son is there whom his father does not discipline?

Hebrews 12:5-7

Household Chores

As members of the family of God, there are expectations that we participate in meaningful ways both personally and corporately. When we were kids, our parents made us do chores around the house. Some of those chores were for personal responsibilities like making our own beds or cleaning up after ourselves. Other chores were for the benefit of the family as a whole like mowing the lawn and washing dishes after dinner. When thinking of the church as a family, let's list some of the personal "chores" as well as some of the corporate "chores."

Personal	Corporate
Study the Scriptures	Teach a Bible study
Pray for yourself and your family	Lead a prayer group to pray for others
Go on a short-term trip	Support a missionary
_____	_____
_____	_____
_____	_____

Privileges and Responsibilities

In addition to the work of the family of God, just like any other family, we also have some privileges. It may be helpful to list some common family activities and draw a comparison to the endeavors we want to see as heirs in the household of God.

Earthly Family	Spiritual Family
Gather together	Attend worship on the weekends
Share meals together	Host a small group meeting
Celebrate life events together	_____
Mourn a loss together	_____
Make decisions together	_____
Care for each other	_____
_____	_____
_____	_____

There is a clear sense that we will hold each other accountable for the growth and benefit of other members of the family. Families are always growing and inviting others to join the family (like in-laws). We learn from and respect older family members, and provide care and direction for younger members. Paul wrote his advice to Timothy in that new church with some helpful comparisons to see the church more as a family instead of just an institution or an organization. He said, "Do not rebuke an older man but encourage him as you would a father, younger men as brothers, older women as mothers, younger women as sisters, in all purity" (1 Timothy 5:1-2).

Tribes

Humans are undoubtedly social creatures. Sociology, anthropology and other sciences have determined that humankind has always existed in community. Tribal circles exist for survival. They are connected through common identities and social structures that maintain order through well-established rules and roles. In their circles, they have privileges and responsibilities just like families because they are extended relations.

In addition to birthright and adoption, the concept of tribes is common in both the Old Testament and the New Testament. The twelve tribes of Israel are merely extended families, and the members identify with each other down through the ages. The book of Revelation records a prophesy that we will see tribes of all people groups gathered together around the throne of God.

After this I looked, and behold, a great multitude that no one could number, from every nation, from all tribes and peoples and languages, standing before the throne and before the Lamb, clothed in white robes, with palm branches in their hands, and crying out with a loud voice, "Salvation belongs to our God who sits on the throne, and to the Lamb!"
Revelation 7:9-10

Since 1974, missiologists have focused their attention on unreached and unengaged people groups, also known as ethno-linguistic tribes. That year, Ralph Winter[2] gave a presentation at the Congress for World Evangelization in Lausanne, Switzerland, which became a seminal moment for global missions. Previously, churches and mission agencies saw the world through the geopolitical lens of nations and political boundaries, but Winter argued we need to prepare our missionary sending force to be more specific in targeting groups of people who share a common identity.

This concept certainly has applications for our own communities as well. Remember when there were different groups in school? There were jocks, nerds, rich kids, poor kids, popular girls, punk boys and the ever-present teacher's pets. All of these groups were gathered in the same school, but they had their own unique identity. They were forming tribes. Even though they were not related by blood, they still had their own unique way of speaking to each other, thinking about education and attending the same functions as a group. When thinking about them theologically, each group would require a different method of

---

2. Ralph Winter, "25 Most Influential Evangelicals", Time Magazine, February 3, 2005.

evangelism. Maybe teamwork concepts would appeal to the jocks. Perhaps the nerds would benefit from having deep conversations regarding complex and philosophical arguments.

Each group has something that serves as a bridge to the gospel that can be discovered by thinking about the ways they relate to each other.

Thinking about tribes may be a helpful substitute for the concept of the family of God, especially when the church is in an area that does not place a high value on families. We rarely hear the terms *brother* and *sister* in many of the local churches we visit in urban areas. Those terms are used more in rural settings where family networks are more stable. In the absence of familial terms, there are ways of relating to each other that provide accountability and vulnerability so that the church will grow deeper spiritually as it grows numerically. Life change can happen when the church seeks to reach people in the groups where they naturally gather.

We have noticed that healthy churches lead their people to reach their tribes with the gospel, instead of breaking up the tribe by separating the members. This is a missiological concept of "extraction." When missionaries on the field see conversions happen, the natural tendency is to extract those persons from their previous social groups and lead them to join this new group—the church. So, they leave their tribe or family in order to form a new tribe or family. Sometimes this is a necessity, particularly in a fundamentalist religious context when they are disowned because of their conversion. But most of the time it is just easier to *leave and join* than it is to *stay and witness*. Some church planting organizations focus on tribal engagement as a strategy by planting churches that are local and native. This means the church may be smaller since it is focused on a specific group, but the tribe already has a shared culture, language and history together. This results in deeper connections with a shared faith in Christ.

For the application of this principle here in the United States, consider the kind of tribes with which we gather: civic clubs, exercise groups, dog park friends, fishing clubs, lake communities, moms of preschoolers, shooting clubs, coin collectors or aviation enthusiasts. The list goes on because, as Western people, we are continually looking for a community of people with which we can relate. Churches that understand our tribal tendencies will implement small groups based on our tribe. Instead of taking people out of these common gatherings to form a new tribe, it would make more sense to form Bible study groups based on these common identities, which will help develop a deeper relationship. The concept of a "church within a church" could mean forming small groups around "tribal" themes. Families with small children could be a tribe. Businesswomen could form a tribe. Single adults, DINKs (Dual Income No Kids) and empty nesters are all tribes or small groups waiting to happen.

The concept of being part of a smaller accountability group within the larger church body can be uncomfortable at first because vulnerability does not come naturally. Having a brother or sister to confide in is just what is needed to overcome some of the obstacles in our lives. The place to find a faithful brother and sister is in the church. For those of us who come from dysfunctional earthly families, we long to be a part of a healthy family or tribe that seeks to love each other unconditionally.

The Lord is building (verb) His church!
It is not a building (noun). It is a people!
A gathered and scattered people
for the sake of the gospel.

Scoring Metric for **The Brotherhood**

This is the fifth in a series of exercises to help your church evaluate its practice of the seven biblical metaphors we explore in this book. Answer the questions below with a rating of 1-5. Add the results together and then divide by 5 to get the score for this chapter on fellowship between members of God's family.

On a scale of 1-5:   Score
1. Are brothers and sisters in Christ dwelling together in unity?   _____
2. Are men and women laboring side-by-side as Paul mentioned in Philippians?   _____
3. Are the concepts of adoption, birthright and inheritance understood?   _____
4. Is there a deep, honest and real fellowship taking place in the congregation?   _____
5. Do the members of God's family know what "chores" they need to do?   _____

Total: _____

÷ 5 = _____

(Record this number in the Appendix under the heading **The Brotherhood**)

THE BROTHERS AND SISTERS

6
THE BULWARK

This Church Sign brings clarity to the church's mission of teaching and preaching the truth of the gospel with a rigorous theology.

... the church of the living God, a pillar and bulwark of the truth.
1 Timothy 3:14-16, NRSV

THE BULWARK

Descriptions of the Church Exemplified by the Bulwark:

- Preaching (9Marks, IMB Foundations)
- Teaching (Purpose Driven Church, IMB Foundations)
- Biblical Theology (9Marks)

"Speaking my truth"
"Disinformation"
"Misinformation"
"Alternative facts"
"Real facts"
"True facts"
"Cold hard facts"
"Indisputable facts"
"False facts"
"Fact check"
"Fact-based"
"Opinion"
"Personal beliefs"
"Personal experience"
"Perception"
"Empirical evidence"
"Erosion of Trust"

Every day, humans discover a new way to dilute the concept of truth. The pace of cultural change is hectic and frenzied, and it is beginning to show instability in every area of life. All of the institutions we have counted on for generations are under enormous stress—education, health care, government, the economy, the media and even the family. We have record low levels of trust in these institutions, and that is especially true of the church.

So, what does the New Covenant church in a post-truth world look like? The short answer is…it looks the same! Since Adam and Eve, the world has always been post-truth. To quote the exasperated preacher in Ecclesiastes:

What has been is what will be,
and what has been done is what will be done,
and there is nothing new under the sun.
Is there a thing of which it is said, "See, this is new"?
It has been already in the ages before us.

Ecclesiastes 1:9-10

Today we have more and more access to information, yet we seem to have less and less understanding. Knowledge increases while wisdom decreases. How can this be?

The preacher of Ecclesiastes summarizes his feelings by admitting, "For in much wisdom is much vexation, and he who increases knowledge increases sorrow" (Ecclesiastes 1:18).

Ecclesiastes is a wonderfully complex piece of wisdom literature. Even the title is challenging to understand. Ecclesiastes is from the Greek word *ekklesia* (an assembly). In the Hebrew Scriptures, the title is *Qoheleth,* which is a feminine form meaning "a female who speaks before the assembly." It is not used anywhere else in Scripture, which leads many scholars to conclude that this book is a personification of Wisdom speaking to a congregation. A subtle nuance here is that this wisdom in Ecclesiastes is being entrusted to an assembly. Even in the Old Testament, there were scholars, teachers and prophets, but without the assembly, they were just "a voice crying out in the wilderness" (Isaiah 40:3).

The biblical assembly (ekklesia) of the New Covenant church is our bulwark for truth. It is the protective barrier that stands between the siege of the world and the people of God who are assembled within its ramparts.

Tradition ascribes authorship of Ecclesiastes to an elderly King Solomon who is best known for his incredible wisdom in the midst of a confusing world. In 1 Kings 3:5, the Lord says to Solomon in a dream, "Ask what I shall give you." This is reminiscent of the tale of a genie in a bottle who will grant someone three wishes. Most people would say, "Long life, wealth and triumph over my enemies." However, Solomon was not like most people because he asked for wisdom. "Give your servant therefore an understanding mind to govern your people, that I may discern between good and evil" (1 Kings 3:9). And because he asked for wisdom from the Lord, his request was honored. In addition to wisdom, the Lord gave him the trifecta of long life, wealth and triumph over his enemies.

Throughout Ecclesiastes, Qoheleth expresses fatigue and frustration through a constant refrain, "I have seen everything that is done under the sun, and behold, all is vanity and a striving after wind" (Ecclesiastes 1:14). The word *vanity* is Hebrew for "vapor" and is sometimes translated as "meaningless" or "futility." We get the sense that an aged King Solomon is profoundly perplexed by the world around him. A man with unlimited knowledge and surrounded by infinite riches is expressing utter confusion. So, he makes his address to the assembly.

Do you feel this way sometimes? Does the world not make sense to you? When you listen to the news, do you find yourself saying something like, "On what planet are we living?" When you visit family for the holidays, are there conflicting opinions around the table? At work, do you find it difficult to understand your colleague's worldview? When your kids come home from school, do they ask you uncomfortable questions?

If you answered yes to any of these, would you find it helpful if you had a group of like-minded friends who made it a priority to seek wisdom from the Lord? That is why it is necessary for the church to be a bulwark of truth—a place of retreat to express vexation, gain insight and improve endurance for the hardships of a post-truth world. We have noticed that the most effective church leaders are those who are unafraid to wrestle with complex and controversial issues. Over the last six years, we have visited hundreds of churches all across the United States and have noticed three ways that church leaders approach the hot topics of our day:

1. "Thus saith the Lord!"
2. "We don't talk about that here."
3. "Let's discuss this further."

No matter the subject (sexuality, war, addiction, politics, identity, migration, globalization and so forth) you will find that the Scriptures speak either directly or indirectly; often with clarity, but sometimes with ambiguity. The easy thing to do is say either, "Thus saith the Lord" or

"We don't talk about that here." But the hard work in a ministry of truth is wrestling with all of the mystery and ambiguity of an ancient text and making it relevant for the complexities of today.

The Apostle Paul instructed his protégé Timothy that part of the mystery of the church is its mission to protect against falsehood. Like the walled cities that defended ancient peoples from enemy attacks, the church is to defend the people of God from the attacks of our spiritual enemy.

I hope to come to you soon, but I am writing these things to you so that, if I delay, you may know how one ought to behave in the household of God, which is the church of the living God, a pillar and buttress [bulwark] of the truth. Great indeed, we confess, is the mystery of godliness:

> *He was manifested in the flesh, vindicated by the Spirit, seen by angels, proclaimed among the nations, believed on in the world, taken up in glory.*

1 Timothy 3:14-16

Bulwark is an old English word that was used to describe a defensive barrier that provided armies with a retreat position for protection. It is used mainly in the King James and New Revised Standard versions of the Bible along with many other military defense terms used as spiritual metaphors like, "strong tower" (Proverbs 18:10), "stronghold" (Psalm 94:22), "fortress" (Psalm 91:2) and "refuge" (Psalm 64:10).

Paul is using this metaphor for the church to instruct Timothy on how to protect God's people who are surrounded by deception. He then provides a synopsis of the truth of the gospel: Jesus appeared in the flesh and conquered death so we can be justified by the Holy Spirit. This act, which was witnessed by angels, was proclaimed to the nations and received by those who would believe. He now sits at God's right hand. That truth is found within the bulwark of the church that Jesus is building.

Indeed, we have a spiritual enemy who uses falsehood as his primary weapon. One day Jesus was speaking to a group of scribes and Pharisees when he said to them:

THE BULWARK

You are of your father the devil, and your will is to do your father's desires. He was a murderer from the beginning, and does not stand in the truth, because there is no truth in him. When he lies, he speaks out of his own character, for he is a liar and the father of lies.

John 8:44

While it is true that we live in a complex world where honesty is rare and deceit is a raging epidemic, there is some comfort in knowing we are not alone. Meeting together as the church of the living God serves as a weekly retreat to take cover from all the attacks of our enemy. During his earthly ministry, Jesus only spoke about the church two times (Matthew 16:18, 18:17). In Matthew 16:18, he used a mysterious military analogy, "And I tell you, you are Peter, and on this rock I will build my church, and the gates of hell shall not prevail against it."

Gates are a defensive position, not an offensive weapon, and yet Jesus described the "gates of hell" as if they were prevailing or advancing. The word *hell* in this passage refers to Hades—a shadowy world of unseen spiritual war that goes on undetected by mortals. Sometimes our English translations use the word hell to describe *gehenna* (the place of eternal torment in Aramaic), but that is not the case here.

In the first century, this message would be clearer than today since they were surrounded by kingdoms with fortresses and gates. Any visit to Europe or other areas of the world that still have the remnants of walled cities you will notice that not all of the walls match. A tour guide will point out, "This wall was built under the rule of *this* king, and that wall was built under *that* king." Kings and kingdoms were always expanding and enlarging their territory. The gates of kingdoms would encroach into new regions with each successive advancement.

We are in a spiritual battle with the kingdom of an unseen enemy who will diligently seek to increase his influence in every area of our lives. Fortunately, the ekklesia serves as our bulwark of truth in a spiritually compromised world.

In Matthew 16:18, Simon receives a new name, Peter, which means "rock" in Greek. Jesus played with words here when he said, "…you are Peter, and on this rock I will build my church." This is when he asked his disciples, "Who do people say I am?" There was some confusion among the many crowds who gathered to hear him teach and watch him perform miracles. Everyone had their own opinion, and most people speculated based on what seemed right in their own eyes. But Peter boldly proclaimed, "You are the Christ, the Son of the living God." And that proclamation was the "rock" upon which the bulwark of the church was established.

Proclaiming vs. Teaching

The Apostle Paul wrote to his emerging church in Corinth to help them as they sought to grow and spread their influence in the Gentile world. He was teaching from a vastly different perspective. Paul was a Hebrew scholar and a Jewish thinker (Philippians 3:4-6), but he was speaking to a Gentile church that existed in a Greco-Roman culture. This passage in 1 Corinthians can help preachers and teachers today as they proclaim the mystery of the gospel in our multicultural settings.

And I, when I came to you, brothers, did not come proclaiming to you the testimony of God with lofty speech or wisdom. For I decided to know nothing among you except Jesus Christ and him crucified. And I was with you in weakness and in fear and much trembling, and my speech and my message were not in plausible words of wisdom, but in demonstration of the Spirit and of power, so that your faith might not rest in the wisdom of men but in the power of God.

Yet among the mature we do impart wisdom, although it is not a wisdom of this age or of the rulers of this age, who are doomed to pass away. But we impart a secret and hidden wisdom of God, which God decreed before the ages for our glory. None of the rulers of this age understood this, for if they had, they would not have crucified the Lord of glory. But, as it is written,

"What no eye has seen, nor ear heard, nor the heart of man imagined, what God has prepared for those who love him" these things God has revealed to us through the Spirit. For the Spirit searches everything,

even the depths of God. For who knows a person's thoughts except the spirit of that person, which is in him? So also no one comprehends the thoughts of God except the Spirit of God. Now we have received not the spirit of the world, but the Spirit who is from God, that we might understand the things freely given us by God. And we impart this in words not taught by human wisdom but taught by the Spirit, interpreting spiritual truths to those who are spiritual.

The natural person does not accept the things of the Spirit of God, for they are folly to him, and he is not able to understand them because they are spiritually discerned. The spiritual person judges all things, but is himself to be judged by no one. "For who has understood the mind of the Lord so as to instruct him?" But we have the mind of Christ.

1 Corinthians 2

Proclamation of the gospel with simplicity is required when addressing those who have not yet surrendered their lives to Christ. Once they cross the threshold of faith, they require *teaching,* which imparts wisdom and hidden mysteries that cannot be understood by "natural" men and women.

The difference between *proclaiming* and *teaching* is helpful to understand as the New Covenant church seeks to reinforce the truth of the gospel. The pastor's sermon during a worship service is often a strategic choice between teaching (*didache*—Greek*)* or proclaiming (*kerygma*—Greek). The teaching ministry of a pastoral leader is important for the growth and development of the church. But there is more to a sermon than just instruction.

When pastors model proclamation for their congregation by preaching or heralding the gospel, believers learn an important skill for when they share the truth of the gospel with their friends, family, coworkers and neighbors. Proclamation of the gospel is a demonstration of the Spirit's power at work in the proclaimer. Just as the Apostle Paul said in 1 Corinthians 2:3-5,

I was with you in weakness and in fear and much trembling, and my speech and my message were not in plausible words of wisdom, but in demonstration of the Spirit and of power, so that your faith might not rest in the wisdom of men but in the power of God.

If we only use persuasive words and wise teaching, then we miss the power of God. Truth is not just what we can prove; that would be the goal of science. Our goal is to reveal those mysteries of God that are left outside the purview of our material world, hidden and waiting to be unveiled through the power of the Spirit's work in and through us.

Teaching is didactic, and teachers seek to inform by using stories that include a moral lesson, systematic order and experiential learning. These lessons probe deeper truths by way of lectures and interactions with students. This allows learners to explore and make applications to their own situations.

Truth or Error

One of the most effective schemes of our spiritual enemy is mixing a little bit of truth with a little bit of error. Something that is false is easy to reject, but the best counterfeits are those that appear to be the real thing. We can look at the world around us and clearly distinguish the differences between other religions of the world and Christianity. Likewise, with just a little biblical knowledge, we can recognize the clear fabrications of cults that seek to attract disgruntled believers. Both of those two groups can be debated and cut off from consideration when looking for the sign of truth in the church.

The problem we are seeking to address in this book is in local churches that may have correct theology and doctrine, but their practice of broadcasting and wrestling with the truth is neglected. Some Christian organizations are merely repositories of the truth, but they refuse to proclaim it. Some are so entrenched within their own bulwarks that they refuse to let anyone in so that they can benefit from its protection. So, we must ask the question, "Why do those buildings with steeples, crosses and bibles even exist?"

The word *church* on the building does not make it the bulwark of truth.

John Stott once said, "An introverted church, turned in on itself, preoccupied with its own survival, has virtually forfeited the right to be the church, for it is denying a major part of its own being."[1]

Doctrinal Statements

Most churches have a doctrinal statement somewhere on their website to describe their faith convictions. They use this document to define the authority that they will subscribe to. Here is an example:

> God has graciously disclosed his existence and power in the created order, and has supremely revealed himself to fallen human beings in the person of his Son, the incarnate Word, Jesus Christ. We believe that God has inspired the words preserved in the Scriptures, the sixty-six books of the Old and New Testaments, which are both record and means of his saving work in the world. These writings alone constitute the verbally inspired Word of God, which is utterly authoritative and without error in the original writings, complete in its revelation of his will for salvation, sufficient for all that God requires us to believe and do, and final in its authority over every domain of knowledge to which it speaks. The Bible is to be believed, as God's instruction, in all that it teaches; obeyed, as God's command, in all that it requires; and trusted, as God's pledge, in all that it promises. As God's people hear, believe, and do the Word, they are equipped as disciples of Christ and witnesses to the gospel.

Notice the action orientation. This is not just a statement with which we can agree, but we are called to act through this declaration. In some statements, you may notice words like "inspired," "infallible" and "inerrant" when it comes to scriptural authority. Sometimes the church

---

1. John Stott, "The Lord Christ is a Missionary Christ", *Declare His Glory*, David M Howard, ed., (Leicester: IVP, 1977), p. 53.

will use the disclaimer "in the original," meaning they are acknowledging the difficulties inherent in translation across language, time and culture. Much time is spent in seminaries to craft and hone the right wording for these statements, and pastors are trained in the art of rightly dividing truth from error. These statements are critical to helping believers understand the purpose of the church.

The problem exists when leaders fail to conclude the debate and start using what they know. We have been in churches that incessantly argue and debate the most minute details of their theology but never put it into practice. Sometimes it felt to us like they were comfortable internalizing the gospel but very uncomfortable externalizing it.

Truth should never be about comfort! If we have a spiritual enemy who seeks to undermine and destroy the truth, by its very nature, the truth will be uncomfortable. Some will say, "The truth of the gospel needs fewer defenders and more proclaimers." Others will argue, "The best offense is a good defense." Either way, being able to trust in a church that will defend the truth regardless of its context is important.

On the opposite extreme, we have seen many churches that blend so seamlessly with the culture that surrounds them that it has no distinctiveness. These churches compromise the truth in an effort to be trendy, modern or relevant. They say and do things that have some semblance of the truth but will often compromise the message of the gospel for the sake of relevance. Truth is an anchor in the storm for believers who are surrounded by the relativism that resides in the prevailing winds of culture.

Indigeneity

Missionaries are trained to translate the timelessness of the gospel into the culture where they are working. Since every group of people exists in a culture, it is important for leaders to study all of the customs, traditions and values surrounding the church — especially when it is their own home territory. The goal is to make the church indigenous while, at the same time, remaining faithful to the truth of the gospel. Indigeneity seeks to consider issues like language, music, dress, food, customs and values so the church will become part of the fabric of that society. In a multicultural region of the world like North America, there are many subtleties and nuances to the culture, so it is only natural to have disagreements. Sometimes truth and culture get mistaken for one another, and that is when conflicts occur.

Most of the church conflicts we see these days are related to culture and preferences but not necessarily related to the truth of the gospel. We wanted to take an outsider's look inside our own church experience and found four relevant "church battles" that exist today—music, preaching style, worship style and decentralization.

Worship music wars are incessant and ongoing in many denominational circles. Most of the time it starts with someone saying, "This is new and I don't like it." Then it builds momentum when enough people "join the chorus" to declare why this new music is not good for the church—it's too loud, too repetitious, too "me" focused and many other similar comments. Then a new voice will emerge as an authoritative opponent who proclaims that this new music is somehow unholy, evil and detrimental to worship. We recall when respectable biblical scholars in the 1980s made claims that drums in the church were anathema. Of course, they used very convincing arguments like historical references to pagan influences, voodoo syncretism and a connection to native rituals. Today, just the mere mention of church music can trigger an impassioned debate like this.

Another battle that exists in churches and church-planting organizations is *topical* versus *expository* preaching styles. Pastors, churches, seminaries and authors have all profited from this very explosive debate in the church. One of the consultation groups we explored for this book is 9Marks. They insist the rightful preaching style for a New Testament church is *expository* because the message content and intent are controlled by the particular passage of scripture in the sermon. On the other side of the argument, *topical* preaching is practiced by church leaders who want to take on the hot topics of the day and find biblical wisdom to make relevant applications. Both of these preaching styles are employed by growing and effective churches all around the world.

One of the most divisive arguments in the church today is the charismatic movement. Some churches attract emotive people, and other churches attract a more stoic audience. We have friends on both sides. Some people have impassioned worship styles and love their charismatic church. They raise their hands, sing at the top of their lungs, dance in the aisles and talk back to their pastor with a hearty, "Amen!" Their theology is quite compatible with our other friends who prefer a more reserved and stoic worship experience in a church that focuses on liturgy. We love to spend time with both friends and can see why God has made them fit his purposes in their various communities.

Another interesting debate that is emerging relates to the house church movement. On the global stage, it is called Disciple Making Movements (DMM) since it is a decentralized movement of indigenous church planting within cell groups. It has a strong appeal, especially among people in nations where Christianity is not well received, as well as in urban areas of the United States. This movement has lots of biblical precedents since all of the first-century early church examples we find in the New Testament follow this model. This is an ongoing debate, and many people are lining up on both sides. Those within the decentralized church movement will refer to the institutional church (ones with buildings, paid pastoral staff and denominations) as "traditional," "legacy" or "predominant" models of church.

All of these things (and many more) are preferences, but the truth of the gospel cannot be compromised for the sake of personal preference and cultural relevancy. Music is cultural. Learning styles (preaching) are cultural. Worship style (emotive or stoic) is cultural. Community is cultural (small/intimate or large/formal). So, once we learn the difference between what is cultural and what is truth, we can see the signs of the bulwark of truth in the church as Christ intended.

Some people within Christianity just want to argue. We all know these people by their fruit—division. These controversialists try to wield truth as a weapon for division instead of using it as a tool for building up and edifying the church. When someone takes a preference and turns it into a reason to divide, we need to heed the advice Paul gave to Timothy.

Remind them of these things, and charge them before God not to quarrel about words, which does no good, but only ruins the hearers. Do your best to present yourself to God as one approved, a worker who has no need to be ashamed, rightly handling the word of truth. But avoid irreverent babble, for it will lead people into more and more ungodliness, and their talk will spread like gangrene. Among them are Hymenaeus and Philetus, who have swerved from the truth, saying that the resurrection has already happened. They are upsetting the faith of some. But God's firm foundation [bulwark] stands, bearing this seal: "The Lord knows those who are his," and, "Let everyone who names the name of the Lord depart from iniquity."

...So flee youthful passions and pursue righteousness, faith, love, and peace, along with those who call on the Lord from a pure heart. Have nothing to do with foolish, ignorant controversies; you know that they breed quarrels. And the Lord's servant must not be quarrelsome but kind to everyone, able to teach, patiently enduring evil, correcting his opponents with gentleness. God may perhaps grant them repentance leading to a knowledge of the truth, and they may come to their senses and escape from the snare of the devil, after being captured by him to do his will. 2 Timothy 2:14-26

There is a difference between arguments and debate. Part of the mystery of the church is seeing both sides of a debate and agreeing to hold two seemingly opposite conclusions in a dynamic tension. If you have not studied theology in an academic setting, these paradoxical truths may make you uncomfortable, but that is okay. Truth is empowering, liberating and sometimes confusing. Truth is like a light that illuminates previously held fallacies that exist in darkness. The hard part is identifying your own personal preferences and comparing them to the truth of the gospel.

The cultural paradox of the New Covenant church of the living God is maintaining a healthy balance between being culturally relevant while also holding firm to the timeless truths of the gospel. Recognizing the difference between culture and truth is a common practice on the mission field in a foreign context, but it is rarely used within one's own culture. With a little intentional effort here at home, the local church can benefit from this mission-field tool of indigeneity.

The truth of the gospel is simple. Over time, God's people have increasingly added more complexity to the church by inserting their own cultural baggage. There will always be disagreements when a group of people gather, but, when conflict begins to take primacy, it is necessary for leaders to return to simplicity. We need the church to be a bulwark of truth and not a house of conflict so God's people can have a place of retreat to endure the spiritual battles that exist in our world.

> **The Lord is building (verb) his church. It is not a building (noun). It is a people! They are a gathered and scattered people for the sake of the gospel.**

Scoring Metric for **The Bulwark**

This is the sixth in a series of exercises to help your church evaluate its practice of the seven biblical metaphors we explore in this book. Answer the questions below with a rating of 1-5. Add the results together and then divide by 5 to get the score for this chapter on teaching and preaching the truth with a rigorous theology. Record your results in the appendix to help you evaluate your congregation's strengths and weaknesses.

On a scale of 1-5:   Score

1. Do leaders discuss ways to proclaim the truth meaningfully with relevance? _____
2. Is truth seen as an anchor in the storm against the prevailing winds of culture? _____
3. Are believers equipped to engage controversy and not avoid discourse? _____
4. Is the church a place of refuge for believers to have substantive dialog? _____
5. Are all the "church battles" resolved or settled? _____

                                                                             Total: _____

                                                                                 ÷ 5 = _____

(Use this number in the Appendix under the heading **The Bulwark**)

❈ 7 ❈
THE BEACON

This Church Sign brings clarity to the church's
mission of cross-cultural impact and global outreach.

You are the light of the world.
Matthew 5:14

Descriptions of the Church Exemplified by the Beacon:

- Missions (IMB Foundations)
- (Purpose Driven Church and 9Marks include global mission under the umbrella of evangelism)

"The light that shines farthest, shines brightest nearest home."

This quote by C.T. Studd, a British missionary to China in the late 1800s, was likely conceived on that slow boat ride from Europe to Asia. All along the coastlines, he would have seen lighthouses that served as signs marking land.

There is something extraordinary about lighthouses. They don't just mark perilous places, but they serve as guides for those who sail in the darkness. The local church serves as a *beacon of light* for a world immersed in darkness. The church whose light shines among the nations shines unusually bright in its own neighborhood!

Light is one of the most subtly used metaphors to describe spiritual conditions in all of Scripture. From Genesis to Revelation, and everywhere in between, biblical writers use *light vs. darkness* to illustrate the transcendent environment between heaven and earth. It all begins with the first few verses of Genesis.

In the beginning, God created the heavens and the earth. The earth was without form and void, and darkness was over the face of the deep. And the Spirit of God was hovering over the face of the waters. And God said, "Let there be light," and there was light. And God saw that the light was good. And God separated the light from the darkness. God called the light Day, and the darkness he called Night. And there was evening and there was morning, the first day.

Genesis 1:1-5

Light is essential for life, so, from the very beginning, the Lord instituted the sun as our source of physical life here on earth. The sun, however, is temporary as we see in the last chapter of our Scriptures when the Lord reclaims his creation by ending darkness.

And night will be no more. They will need no light of lamp or sun, for the Lord God will be their light, and they will reign forever and ever.
Revelation 22:5

Until that day, our existence is marked by our need for light. Jesus was prophesied by the prophet Isaiah as the "great light" who will come and illuminate the darkness of mankind.

The people who walked in darkness have seen a great light; those who dwelt in a land of deep darkness, on them has light shone.
Isaiah 9:2

A few verses later in Isaiah 9:6, the coming Messiah is announced (which George Frideric Handel used in the chorus of his amazing oratorio *Messiah*).

For to us a child is born, to us a son is given,
and the government will be on his shoulders.
And he will be called
Wonderful Counselor, Mighty God,
Everlasting Father, Prince of Peace.

The Gospel of John, which opens like an epic symphony of words, retells the story of creation with new insight into the Messiah's presence and role, as well as his mission to bring light to the people of God.

In the beginning was the Word, and the Word was with God, and the Word was God. He was in the beginning with God. All things were made through him, and without him was not any thing made that was made. In him was life, and the life was the light of men. The light shines in the darkness, and the darkness has not overcome it.
John 1:1-5

When we study the life and ministry of Jesus, his incarnation serves as a perfect model for the church. He lived among those who dwelled in spiritual darkness on earth, so his light would shine and give them clarity of purpose.

The nature of light is to shine, and its purpose is to dispel darkness. However, light that shines in lighted places is sometimes thoughtless, careless, wasteful, extravagant and cavalier. Ask any mother how many times she has to remind her kids to turn off the lights during the day. However, the light that shines in darkened places serves as a sign of purpose to all who see the light. Jesus said His followers are the "light of the world."

You are the light of the world. A city set on a hill cannot be hidden. Nor do people light a lamp and put it under a basket, but on a stand, and it gives light to all in the house. In the same way, let your light shine before others, so that they may see your good works and give glory to your Father who is in heaven.

Matthew 5:14-16

So, if we are the light of the world, what is the ultimate purpose of the church as custodians, guardians and caretakers of the lighthouse? We are to SHINE! We are to shine far and bright! That is our *Missio Dei*, the mission of God to shine the light of the gospel message into a world filled with spiritual darkness.

Missio Dei

Unfortunately, very few churches have an intentional strategy in place with a focus on shining their lights into darkened places, which are inhabited by unreached people.[1] Many churches approach cross-cultural missions rather cavalierly. This was true of most mid-twentieth-century churches that operated under a popular philosophy known as *missio ecclesiae* or "mission of the church." This Latin phrase meant that a church could authorize itself to set its own mission parameters. In a meeting of the International Missionary Council in 1952, Dr. Karl Hartenstein proposed the phrase Missio Dei as a corrective statement to the cavalier approach of churches, which made missions "in the image of

---

1. "The Future of Missions," (Barna Group, 2020) pg. 17

man." Two decades later, Billy Graham, John Stott, Ralph Winter and other mission thinkers organized a gathering around this idea at the International Conference on World Evangelization at Lausanne, Switzerland.[2] Now known as the Lausanne Movement, they seek to connect influencers and ideas for global missions, which include missionary sending agencies, churches, parachurch organizations and non-governmental organizations from all nations.

Rather than every local church doing what was *right in their own eyes*, this linking of resources helps unite all believers under a unified banner of world evangelization. They seek to make the mission of God more intentional and proactive in theology as well as methodology.

It is impossible to read the Scriptures and study the life of Christ and his followers and walk away without the impression that the church has a divine mandate to be proactive and intentional about taking the gospel message to all of the world. Some pastors and church leaders have found ways of avoiding this imperative, only to miss the entire point of the final instructions that Jesus gave after his resurrection and before his ascension. Those instructions are called the Great Commission, and they were our marching orders by our King of kings so the church would serve as his ambassadors sent to accomplish his purposes until he returns.

Sometimes church leaders will prioritize the *institution* of the church over the *mission* of the church. The Missio Dei must be our priority, not the missio ecclesiae. Without the mission, there is no need for the church. Chris Wright, an Anglican missiologist says it this way,

> It is not so much the case that God has a mission for his church in the world, [but] that God has a church for his mission in the world. Mission was not made for the church; the church was made for mission—God's mission.[3]

The church serves as a beacon of hope for people who are spiritually lost in hard-to-reach places in the world. This clarification of the Missio

---

2. Lusanne Movement, 1974, https://lausanne.org/our-legacy (accessed March 30, 2024)
3. Christopher Wright, "The Mission of God's People: A Biblical Theology of the Church's Mission" (Grand Rapids: Zondervan 2006), pg. 54

Dei was preceded by the launch of the modern missionary movement by pioneers like William Carey to India, David Livingstone to Africa, Hudson Taylor to China and many others in the late eighteenth and early nineteenth centuries.

There was a great spiritual awakening in Europe and North America during that time, and the Lord began calling missionaries from those churches to take the gospel message into uncharted territories. These early missionaries pioneered strategies like Bible translation in local languages, cross-cultural education, communication, medical interventions, evangelism and church planting. They also were instrumental in eliminating horrific customs like "widow burning" in India (burning the wife alive along with the cremation of her dead husband's body). In Africa, missionaries exposed the error of "twin burning." Witch doctors taught that twin babies were a curse, so they were killed and the mother was shunned from the tribe. Everywhere these pioneers went, they improved the lives of people living in darkness.

Imago Dei

Education and healthcare taken around the globe by missionaries have undeniably changed the world, but those were just tools and strategies for the principal work of a missionary. The most important part of their work was introducing people to the concept of *Imago Dei*—the foundation of human nature that we were created in the image of an Almighty God. And because we were born in his image, we are to join him in his purpose of being light in the darkness.

To accept the calling to be "the light of the world" implies a willingness to live and work in spiritually dark places! Unlike other signs of the church, there is no mystery in this Great Commission. Jesus was not vague when he commissioned his followers to be witnesses of the gospel to the world. And no presentation of the gospel is complete without the imperative Jesus gave to his followers after his resurrection and before his ascension into heaven. This Great Commission mandate was given by Jesus in the New Testament five different times in five different places to five different groups of people during those forty days —John 20:21; Mark 16:15; Matthew 28:18-20; Luke 24:44-49; Acts 1:7-8 (in chronological order).

Marvin Newell, in his book *Commissioned*, describes this divine charter that Jesus gave to his church as a critically essential piece of our existence. He says, "Without question, these five mission statements of Jesus make up the missional Magna Carta of the church, from its inception, for today, and into the future."[4] These were the last requests and final instructions by Jesus of what his church should be doing until he returns.

There is no hidden message or ambiguity. We don't need a special degree in the original languages to interpret a deeper meaning. It is straightforward and clear.

The fact that Jesus gave these instructions so consistently and regularly during that interim timeframe should give us cause for deep investments in our churches. So much so, that, before we do anything else, we should be doing these things as listed in the five Great Commission statements: going, making disciples, baptizing, teaching, proclaiming, sending, expecting to receive power and witnessing to all nations, in all the world, to the ends of the earth, until the end of the age. For a comprehensive look at how the local church can develop a missionary pipeline through strategic partnerships with other Great Commission organizations, see our book *Pipeline*.[5]

Some church leaders have justified their lack of global engagement by saying, "Our church is surrounded by needs right here in our own neighborhood. Once our light shines bright here, *then* we will go to the nations." That sounds reasonable, but it is unrealistic that any church will ever get to the place where it has completely evangelized an entire community to a satisfactory degree. That is a bad excuse to ignore the Lord's mandate. For this reason, we would like to introduce you to an important Greek word—*kai*. As a part of speech, it is a conjunction that joins the nouns in Acts 1:8, an important Great Commission statement.

---

4. Marvin Newell, Commissioned: What Jesus Wants You to Know as You Go (Church Smart Resources, 2010) 28.
5. David and Lorene Wilson, Pipeline: Engaging the Church in Missionary Mobilization (Littleton: William Carey Press, 2018)

These are the very last words spoken by Jesus as he was ascending into heaven.

But you will receive power when the Holy Spirit has come upon you, and **kai** *you will be my witnesses in Jerusalem and* **kai** *in all Judea and* **kai** *Samaria, and* **kai** *to the end of the earth." And when he had said these things, as they were looking on, he was lifted up, and a cloud took him out of their sight.*

Acts 1:8-9

Notice there is no paradox to discuss here either. He did not say "and *then*" with an implication to finish one region at a time with exclusivity, but he simply said "and," meaning simultaneously with inclusivity. Jesus gave his followers a dynamic and strategic imperative for mission engagement in four regional concentric circles. Jerusalem is in the center and moving out toward Judea, and Samaria and all the way to the farthest reaches of humanity on earth.

Don't be Like the Early Church!

Even though the early church in Jerusalem heard this imperative from Jesus directly in Acts 1:8, they did not act upon it until Acts 8:1 when persecution broke out and forced them to scatter.

... And there arose on that day a great persecution against the church in Jerusalem, and they were all scattered throughout the regions of Judea and Samaria ... Now **those who were scattered went about preaching the word.** Acts 8:1-4

Jesus gave his commission to the church in Acts 1:8, but the church was reluctant to leave the relative comfort and security of their hometown, so he made their hometown uncomfortable and unsafe in Acts 8:1.

Contemporary church leaders frequently use the activities spelled out in Acts 2 to organize their ministry. It is a good list of ministries and checks all the boxes of what most local churches consider to be necessary for a wholistic ministry. Read through the list and see if this early church is missing anything compared to the final words of the Lord Jesus.

And they devoted themselves to the apostles' **teaching** *and the* **fellowship**, *to the* **breaking of bread** *and the* **prayers**. *And awe came upon every soul, and many* **wonders and signs** *were being done through the apostles. And all who believed were* **together** *and had all things in common. And they were selling their possessions and belongings and* **distributing the proceeds** *to all, as any had* **need**. *And day by day,* **attending the temple** *together and* **breaking bread** *in their homes, they received their food with glad and generous hearts,* **praising God** *and having favor with all the people. And* **the Lord added to their number** *day by day those who were being saved. [Emphasis mine.]*
Acts 2:42-47

Did you notice anything missing? This list of activities is missing the commission from Acts 1:8 to go and be witnesses in places *outside* of Jerusalem.

The book of Acts is a historical account of the early church. Many biblical scholars will warn against reading Acts *prescriptively*, meaning as a book of doctrine and practice, but, rather, we are encouraged to read it *descriptively*, as a description of what happened.

The activities of the church recorded in Acts 2 are not meant to be an exhaustive *prescriptive* list, but they are a *descriptive* list of what happened. And ironically, even though these activities are good, they are incomplete. They lack an emphasis on the church actively going to Judea, Samaria and the ends of the earth as witnesses of the gospel message.

Jesus gave the church a commission in Acts 1:8, but, instead, the church decided to just do Acts 2:42, so the Lord enacted Acts 8:1.

When Everything is Missions

Intuitively, most Christ followers know missions are important, but without a complete biblical definition, there exists the possibility for unhealthy and potentially deceptive practices. We have heard of churches that call everything they do missions. For many reasons, this is problematic since it impacts the church budget and calendar and has the potential for gospel impact around the world. Financially, a church may label something in its budget as missions so people will give more money toward that line item. Additionally, a church may identify local ministry projects as missions so people will get more involved. Local projects would be better labeled as ministry or outreach, but those words do not carry the influential impact of the word missions.

A missionary friend shared his testimony about when he was beginning to sense the Lord leading his family to serve overseas on the mission field. He made an appointment with his pastor to talk about that calling. During their meeting, the pastor said to him, "Why would you go all the way around the world when you can be a missionary to your own neighborhood? You don't even need to learn a new language to do it!" Thankfully, this missionary didn't listen to his pastor because he knew the Lord was preparing him to serve Muslims, learn Arabic and be a beacon of light to people who do not have the luxury of neighborhoods filled with lighthouses. This pastor had no vision for the church being the *light of the world* and putting it on a stand to give light to all of the house. He wanted to keep this missionary light *under his own basket*. Matthew Ellison and Denny Spitters wrote an amazing book that discusses the difficulties that exist in a church—*When Everything is Missions*.[6]

---

6. M. Ellison and D. Spitters, When Everything is Missions (Bottomline Media, 2017)

From Seating Capacity to Sending Capacity

Healthy churches often focus on seating capacities in their buildings to accommodate growth. However, Rick Warren, J. D. Greer, Mike Stachura and other pastors have reminded us that we should measure the health of a church by its sending capacity, not by its seating capacity. A *good* pastor wants to leave a legacy in his local community, and that is a noble pursuit. But *great* pastors leave legacies all around the world! For an in-depth look at this transition, read *Gaining by Losing: Why the Future Belongs to Churches that Send* by J.D. Greear.[7]

The Church at Antioch

There is a first-century church like that in the Book of Acts. The church at Antioch took the last words of Jesus seriously, and we are recipients of their impact today because they were intentional and proactive as a beacon of light, making Christ known among the nations.

Now there were in the church at Antioch prophets and teachers, Barnabas, Simeon who was called Niger, Lucius of Cyrene, Manaen a lifelong friend of Herod the tetrarch, and Saul. While they were worshiping the Lord and fasting, the Holy Spirit said, "Set apart for me Barnabas and Saul for the work to which I have called them." Then after fasting and praying they laid their hands on them and sent them off.
Acts 13:1-3

This story begins with church leaders worshiping and fasting—two activities that represent both spiritual and physical actions. They are demonstrations of corporate behavior, which led them to discern the will of God. The church leaders gave serious thought and consideration to all of the implications as they were surrendering to the will of God for their

---

7. J. D. Greear, Gaining by Losing: Why the Future belongs to Churches that Send (Grand Rapids: Zondervan, 2016)

church. Paul and Barnabas had previously received their call from the Lord, and this was the event where the church affirmed that calling to go to the Gentiles.

When these church leaders "laid their hands on them," they were communicating to Paul and Barnabas, "We are a part of you, and you are a part of us." This had profound implications on the sincerity of the local church as they ordained and commissioned their own people to go into far-off distant places. Today, pastors, elders and missionaries follow in this same lineage of passing the mantle from one generation to the next by ceremonially "laying on hands" to ordain and commission. It is a continuation of this event in the life of the church at Antioch.

The last activity recorded in this church commissioning service is important and should not be missed. It is a brief, seemingly add-on phrase: "sent them off." These missionaries likely needed many things as they headed out on a cross-cultural journey—money for travel expenses, advice from other travelers on local customs, care for family members who were being left behind and much more. We don't know from this text what all the church did for Paul and Barnabas, but we know missionaries today have a great many needs as well. That is why we wrote a book entitled *Mind the Gaps: Engaging the Church in Missionary Care.*[8] There are many resources available for church leaders who would like to take good care of their "sent ones". But resources are of no use unless a church has a proactive and intentional plan to light up a world filled with spiritual darkness.

It is exciting for a church to send missionaries. It can be even more energizing when the missionary returns with news of the Lord's activity in distant lands. The church at Antioch did not just send and forget Paul and Barnabas; they were intimately involved in prayer, care and celebration when they returned.

When they had preached the gospel to that city and had made many disciples, they returned to Lystra and to Iconium and to Antioch, strengthening the souls of the disciples, encouraging them to continue in the faith, and saying that through many tribulations we must enter the

---

8. David J. Wilson, Mind the Gaps: Engaging the Church in Missionary Care (Believers Press, 2015)

kingdom of God. And when they had appointed elders for them in every church, with prayer and fasting they committed them to the Lord in whom they had believed.

... and from there they sailed to Antioch, where they had been commended to the grace of God for the work that they had fulfilled. And when they arrived and gathered the church together, they declared all that God had done with them, and how he had opened a door of faith to the Gentiles. And they remained no little time with the disciples.

Acts 14:21-28

One of the biggest needs for a missionary today is to be allowed to share the story of their adventures with their sending church. At the end of Acts chapter 14, we see that Paul and Barnabas returned to Antioch with many encouraging stories of all the Lord did through them among the Gentiles. They proclaimed the gospel, they were persecuted yet they endured, and they set up churches with leaders all along their journey. And don't miss that very last sentence, "And they remained *no little time* with the disciples" The church at Antioch did not just give them three minutes of stage time during a Sunday service! It takes time, *sacrificial time*, to be the beacon of light in a dark world. Neal Pirolo provides incredible resources for churches that want to send and receive missionaries well in two of his books: *Serving as Senders*[9] and *The Reentry Team*.[10]

The Apostle Paul (a missionary who was sent out by the church at Antioch) described his calling through the church to the Gentiles.

Of this gospel I was made a minister according to the gift of God's grace, which was given me by the working of his power. To me, though I am the very least of all the saints, this grace was given, to preach to the Gentiles the unsearchable riches of Christ, and to bring to light for everyone what is the plan of the mystery hidden for ages in God, who created all things, so that through the church the manifold wisdom of God might now be made known to the rulers and authorities in the

---

9. Neal Pirolo, Serving as Senders: How to Care for your Missionaries (ERI, 1991)
10. Neal Pirolo, The Reentry Team: Caring for your Returning Missionaries (ERI, 2000)

heavenly places. This was according to the eternal purpose that he has realized in Christ Jesus our Lord, in whom we have boldness and access with confidence through our faith in him. So I ask you not to lose heart over what I am suffering for you, which is your glory.

Ephesians 3:7-13

Contextualization

Missionaries like the Apostle Paul develop a set of skills that can be beneficial for their sending church. After Paul and Barnabas debriefed with the church at Antioch in Acts 14, they were sent to the church in Jerusalem to address a critical issue with church leaders in Acts 15 regarding reaching the Gentiles. They used their missionary journey lessons to help guide and shape the direction of that home church.

Today, our local churches in North America can benefit from studying missiological strategies gleaned from our cross-cultural workers as well. The Upstream Collective offers excellent resources for the local church that desires to use missiological principles to reach their world for Christ. One of their books is called *Tradecraft*.[11] When a church studies its own community through a missiological lens, it gains a new and fresh perspective. Concepts such as contextualization, mapping, indigenous, person of peace, exegeting culture and more are explored and applied to the local church here in North America.

One often helpful concept is the *contextualization of culture*. When a church exists in a culture that is familiar to church leaders, they can easily forget to make the church appropriately relevant to their own culture. This, however, is a double-edged sword. When a church is irrelevant, it may not grow. But if a church is too relevant, then it may not be effective. Consider these cultural examples from church planting on the mission field in the Middle East: dress, music and language.

In a Muslim context, missionaries seek to wear clothes that match the customs of the culture. Their church music may reflect the style and modes of that culture also. And finally, using the local language in the

---

11. Larry McCrary, *Tradecraft: For the Church on Mission* (Upstream Collective, 2017)

church is important for validation and adaptation. All of these things can be considered culturally relevant for the sake of effectively representing the church of that culture.

However, what are the limitations of relevancy? Perhaps, wearing the symbol of Islam, the crescent, instead of the cross? Maybe singing songs from the Quran instead of songs about Jesus? What about interpreting the Bible into Arabic in a way that minimizes the doctrines of Christianity to make it more palatable for Muslim Background Believers (MBB)? Determining where the lines of contextualization are in a foreign context may help the local church in North America determine its own boundaries.

Missiologists wrestle with "contextual adaptation," by using the C-scale of contextualization (C1 – C6). When you are thinking about being "the light of the world," how much compromise can occur before the gospel proclamation is irrelevant?

In a foreign context, C1 may look like the missionary's home church with little to no adaptation at all. Even though the church is in another country with another language and culture, a C1 church may reflect the sending nation rather than the receiving nation. An example would be hosting a worship service in English when all the attendees only speak Arabic.

C2 adaptation would interpret the church services in the local language. However, it would translate the hymns so the words were recognizable, but the tune, melodies and mode would remain the same as that of the missionary's home base. An example would be performing translated hymns in India but, instead of playing an Indian sitar, the church uses a Western-style guitar. Even though the lyrics are translated, the tune and style are still foreign.

C3 adaptation alters the music to match the surrounding cultural norms, and the missionary makes the effort to conform to the local style of appearance and customs. The mission team learns the local language, wears the native dress and finds musicians who are skilled in popular cultural music with words and poetic concepts that are translated from the original biblical sources. New hymns and songs are created using culturally relevant symbology from the nation's history.

This is the midpoint of contextualization and a place where most mission thinkers find agreement. The C4 level of adaptation takes a turn to start incorporating local religious practices to infuse meaning that is significant for the host culture. In the example of a missionary in a Muslim context, MBBs may maintain their Islamic prayer rituals but exchange the content of their prayers with Christian wording. The word scholars use here is *syncretism*, which is not always good, but can be justified when appropriate. Before we condemn this on the mission field, we need to look within our own church culture in North America.

Our two favorite seasons, Christmas and Easter, are essentially syncretistic. We have no evidence to support that Jesus was born on December 25. It is likely that Northern European Christians adapted this holiday tradition to coincide with the pagan celebration of the winter solstice. Similarly, Easter originated from a pagan festival marking the spring equinox, a celebration of new life. These are not necessarily wrong, but cults have emerged by using these syncretistic practices to draw skeptical Christians away from the church.

The remaining contextualization scales—C5 (insider movements) and C6 (secret believers)—reflect little to no differentiation from the surrounding culture. They remain tucked comfortably within their culture, traditions, mores, values and social norms.

The debate here is complex and unsettled. On one side, practitioners advocate for Jesus only, no church, no religious Christianity, no institutional accountability, only Jesus. Of course, there is no biblical argument, but there are certainly practical realities that make Insider Movements and Secret Believers something to research. Exposure has caused missionaries in closed-access nations to have their visas revoked, and they are deported out of the country. This is even worse for nationals since they face rejection by their families, imprisonment and even execution. Some missiologists would argue that hidden believers can still be light in the darkness marked by their obscurity.

On the other side of this debate, adherents believe the church is meant to have a visible impact. It should not be concealed from the world in secret. As Jesus said about his church,

You are the light of the world. A city set on a hill cannot be hidden. Nor do people light a lamp and put it under a basket, but on a stand, and it gives light to all in the house. In the same way, let your light shine before others, so that they may see your good works and give glory to your Father who is in heaven.

Matthew 5:14-16

Those on this side of the debate will summarize that there is no such thing as covert Christianity or clandestine discipleship. The grave reality, according to Open Doors,[12] is that, in 2022, more than 360 million Christians around the world experienced "high levels of persecution and discrimination." They also estimate the number of Christians martyred that year was 5,898.

While that is the reality in which missionaries must work today, those conditions do not exist here in North America. The only conundrum we are faced with as the North American church prepares for global cross-cultural engagement is a clear determination to accept the risk inherent in international missions work. Along with risk, there must be appropriate preparation for those who, like Paul and Barnabas, are called to go. The sending church would do well to conduct regular rehearsals for worst-case scenarios as part of sending them well. The Apostle John applauds this kind of missionary support.

Beloved, it is a faithful thing you do in all your efforts for these brothers, strangers as they are, who testified to your love before the church. You will do well to send them on their journey in a manner worthy of God. For they have gone out for the sake of the name, accepting nothing from the Gentiles. Therefore we ought to support **people like these, that we may be fellow workers for the truth.**

3 John 1:5-8

The contrast of being light in a spiritually dark world is inescapable for any church that studies Scripture and is faithful to its teaching. If an organization you are attending calls itself a church but does not demonstrate this "sign of the church," then you can be like Paul and

---

12. www.Opendoors.org, continuously updated, accessed March 30, 2024.

Barnabas as they spoke boldly to religious leaders of their day, "...the Lord has commanded us, saying, 'I have made you a light for the Gentiles, that you may bring salvation to the ends of the earth'" (Acts 13:47).

> **The word *church* on the building does not make it the Church of the Living God, which shines the light of Christ in the neighborhood and among the nations.**

This church sign of being a beacon of light is not something that can be manufactured or manmade. Our light is merely a reflection from the Lord. In the Old Testament, the skin of Moses reflected the glory of the Lord when he met with God on the mountain.

When Moses came down from Mount Sinai, with the two tablets of the testimony in his hand as he came down from the mountain, Moses did not know that the skin of his face shone because he had been talking with God. Aaron and all the people of Israel saw Moses, and behold, the skin of his face shone, and they were afraid to come near him ... And when Moses had finished speaking with them, he put a veil over his face.
Exodus 34:29-30, 33

The Apostle Paul used this moment in the history of Israel to teach the church of the New Covenant about our calling to be light in this world.

And we all, with unveiled face, beholding the glory of the Lord, are being transformed into the same image from one degree of glory to another. For this comes from the Lord who is the Spirit.
2 Corinthians 3:18

Churches that behold the Light of the World will become a reflection of his light in the world. In these churches, it becomes natural to bring regular attention to the needs around the globe with the purpose of shining their light into the darkness. There will be interest in global affairs, but, more than that, there will be strategic interventions that turn tragedies into opportunities to be bearers of the light. The church that is engaged in praying for the nations will see their prayers answered because light dispels darkness, and darkness can never overcome the light.

**The Lord is building (verb) his church.
It is not a building (noun). It is a people!
They are a gathered and scattered
people for the sake of the gospel.**

Scoring Metric for **The Beacon**

This is the last in a series of exercises to help your church evaluate its practice of the seven biblical metaphors we explore in this book. Answer the questions below with a rating of 1-5. Add the results together and then divide by 5 to get the score for this chapter on cross-cultural impact and global outreach. Record your results in the appendix to help you evaluate your congregation's strengths and weaknesses.

On a scale of 1-5:   Score
1. Does the light of your church shine to the nations? _____
2. Is the mission of the church clearly defined including cross-cultural outreach? _____
3. Does your church have a proactive plan to mobilize missionaries? _____
4. Does your church have an intentional missionary care strategy? _____
5. Is the church prepared to accept the risks inherent in global evangelization? _____

                                                                         Total: _____
                                                                            $\div 5 =$ _____

(Use this number in the Appendix under the heading **The Beacon**)

CONCLUSION

The word *church* on the building does not make it the church of the Living God that Jesus died for, was raised for and will come back for when he returns. His church was established to accomplish *his* mission on earth as ambassadors of a kingdom, not of this world. The mission of worshipping (Bride) our Creator and serving our neighbors (Body) can only be accomplished as the church abides in his presence (Branches) to bear witness as the living temple (Building) that he is building in us as its living stones. When we live together in unity as a heavenly family (Brothers and Sisters) we are fortified by his truth (Bulwark) against the spiritually compromised world that surrounds us. We are called to reflect his light (Beacon) into our neighborhoods and among the nations.

The church today needs to reach back and rediscover mystery and paradoxical thinking as it seeks to influence a very complex world. When missionaries enter an unfamiliar culture, they carry with them a toolbox filled with tools that help them decipher the traditions, customs and values so they can decode and interpret the gospel into that society. Our local churches need to use these tools because they are finding themselves as strangers and aliens in a rapidly changing world. Ideas found in *ethnomusicology* can help the church stay relevant in their worship. *Servant leadership* still attracts people because it is effective and demonstrates selflessness. A *theology of risk and suffering* gives

CONCLUSION

Christ-followers a vision for trust and reliance on God when everyone else is trusting in themselves. S*yncretism* can be found in every church when the values of society are allowed to flourish without restraint. However, by using missionary tools, churches can be strategic and intentional to find things in their culture that will make the church *indigenous* while keeping a focus on influencing the society, rather than being influenced by it. One of the most effective ways to do this is *engaging the tribes* that already exist in a community and *contextualizing* the gospel message for each successive generation.

The first-century church was known for its extraordinary ways of living and dying. Perhaps we can learn from their example as described in this excerpt from the *Letter to Diognetus*:[1]

> There is something extraordinary about their lives. They live in their own countries as though they were passing through. They play their full role as citizens, but labor under all of the disabilities of aliens. Any country can be their homeland but for them their homeland, wherever it may be, is a foreign country. ... They live in the flesh, but they are not governed by the desires of the flesh. They pass their days upon earth, but they are citizens of heaven. Obedient to the laws, they yet live on a level that transcends the law. Christians love all, but all persecute them. Condemned because they are not understood, they are put to death, but raised to life again. They live in poverty but enrich many. They are totally destitute but possess an abundance of everything. They suffered dishonor, but that is their glory. They are defamed but vindicated. A blessing is their answer to abuse, deference their response to insult. For the good they do, they receive the punishment of malefactors, but even then, they rejoice, as though receiving the gift of life.

In more recent history, Deitrich Bonhoeffer served as an example of a man who stood firm in his faith against the complicity of an institutional church that lost its way in a confusing world. During the Nazi era in Germany, the state-sponsored church became preoccupied with survival during that nation's time of crisis. Decisions were made for the sake of saving the institution, not as representatives of God's

---

1. *"Letter to Diognetus"* www.vatican.va, continuously updated, accessed 3/30/2024.

CONCLUSION

Kingdom on earth. They not only kept their silence against the atrocities happening in their nation, but they participated in it when they allowed the state to influence their doctrines. Church leaders adopted what was known as the "Aryan Paragraph" thinking it would save them and preserve the institution. Thankfully the "Religion-less Christianity"[2] espoused by Bonhoeffer endured as a remnant of the church at the time but at a great cost. The life of Bonhoeffer was sacrificed on the altar of that institutional church.

Institutions are manmade organizations that are established for the protection and endurance of the entity. On the surface, that is a good thing. We all benefit from institutions like schools, hospitals, governments, economies and even the institutions of marriage and family. These pillars of society help us make sense of things and understand the world that surrounds us.

However, an over-emphasis on the institution of the church only serves to reduce its infinite mystery. That reductionist way of thinking is counter to the paradox we have been taught by our Lord when he said, "If anyone would come after me, let him deny himself and take up his cross and follow me. For whoever would save his life will lose it, but whoever loses his life for my sake and the gospel's will save it" (Mark 8:34-35).

Therefore, the church is a gathering of individuals who have chosen to follow Jesus in this way so they can live out this mystery and paradox in concert with one another. H. Richard Niebuhr wrote this in his book *The Paradox of Church and World:*[3]

> Ultimately, the problem of church and world involves us in a paradox; unless the church accommodates itself to the world, it becomes sterile inwardly and outwardly; unless it transcends the world, it becomes indistinguishable from the world and loses its effectiveness no less surely. ... The rhythm of approach and withdrawal need not be like the swinging of the pendulum, mere repetition without progress; it may be more like the rhythm of the waves that wash upon the beach; each

---

2. Eberhard Bethge, Dietrich Bonhoeffer: A Biography (Fortress Press; rev. ed. 2000)
3. Jon Diefenthaler, The Paradox of Church and World: Selected Writings of H. Richard Niebuhr (Fortress Press, 2015)

CONCLUSION

succeeding wave advances a little farther into the world with its cleansing gospel before that gospel becomes sullied with the earth.

Metaphors for the church were used by New Testament writers to set our minds on "things that are above, not on things that are on earth" (Colossians 3:2). We need more mystery and paradoxical thinking, despite the messiness that ensues. The church today is too sterile with its sixty-minute worship formats, risk-averse policies and procedures, bullet point observations of spiritual formation and the fear of suffering for our faith. Living safe and secure lives inside of our community fortresses was not the plan Jesus gave in his Great Commission. At some point, there will be a reckoning, and shepherds will need to give an account of how they led their flocks (yet another metaphor that needs to be examined).

We hope church leaders will use these metaphors as tools for evaluating the condition of their organizations, and that church planters will use them to design their newly-burgeoning churches. May the Lord reveal things that are hidden, covered up, mysterious, and hard to understand to a new generation of faithful church leaders, for the sake of the gospel in all the world and to future generations.

APPENDIX

At the end of each chapter, you will find a list of questions with a scoring metric. Enter those results here and then add them to the radar graph below to visually demonstrate the areas of strengths and weaknesses that may be hidden in your church.

Your Church

Chapter	Score
The Bride	_____
The Body	_____
The Branches	_____
The Building	_____
The Brotherhood	_____
The Bulwark	_____
The Beacon	_____

Example for the "First Bapticostal Mennoterian Church"

Chapter	Score
The Bride	4
The Body	3
The Branches	4
The Building	2
The Brotherhood	4
The Bulwark	5
The Beacon	2

BIBLIOGRAPHY

Foundations: International Mission Board. "www.store.imb.org/imb-foundations" (accessed 2023).

Bethge, Eberhard. *Dietrich Bonhoeffer: A Biography.* Fortress Press, 2000.

Dever, Mark. *9Marks of a Healthy Church.* Center for Church Reform, 2001.

Diefenthaler, Jon. *The Paradox of Church and World: Selected Writings of H. Richard Niebuhr.* Fortress Press, 2015.

Ellison, Matthew and Denny Spitters. *When Everything is Missions.* Bottomline, 2017.

Greear, J.D. *Gaining by Losing: Why the Future belongs to Churches that Send.* Zondervan, 2015.

Howard, David M, *Declare His Glory.* IVP, 1977.

McCrary, Larry, et al. *Tradecraft: For the Church on Mission.* Upstream Collective, 2017.

Nelson, Tom. *Work Matters: Connection Sunday Worship to Monday Work.* Crossway, 2021.

Newell, Marvin. *Commissioned: What Jesus Wants You to Know as You Go.* ChurchSmart, 2010.

Pirolo, Neal. *Serving as Senders: How to Care for your Missionaries.* Emmaus Road International, 1991.

Pirolo, Neal. *The Reentry Team: Caring for your Returning Missionaries.* Emmaus Road International, 2001.

Stott, John. www.johnstott.org/work/urbana-the-lord-christ-is-a-missionary-christ (accessed 2023)

Warren, Rick. *The Purpose Driven Church: Growth Without Compromising Your Message & Mission.* Zondervan, 1995.

Wilkinson, Bruce. *Secrets of the Vine: Breaking Through to Abundance.* Multnomah, 2002.

Wilson, David J. *Mind the Gaps: Engaging the Church in Missionary Care.* Believers Press, 2015.

BIBLIOGRAPHY

Wilson, David and Lorene. *Pipeline: Engaging the Church in Missionary Mobilization.* William Carey, 2018

Wilson, David and Lorene. *Transforming Missionaries: A Short-Term Mission Guide.* Three Strand Partners, 2007.

Wright, Christopher. *The Mission of God's People: A Biblical Theology of the Church's Mission.* Zondervan, 2006.

ABOUT THE AUTHORS

David and Lorene Wilson are partners in ministry and have served together in missions in the local church since 1995. Dave has a MDiv from New Orleans Baptist Theological Seminary and a DMin from Campbell University. Lorene has a BA in Religious Studies from Mercer University and an AAS in Office Administration from Clayton State College.

They are passionate about providing resources that will encourage and equip the church, agency and missionary to partner together in fulfilling the Great Commission. Other books written by the Wilsons include:

Transforming Missionaries: A Short-Term Mission Guide
Mind the Gaps: Engaging the Church in Missionary Care
Pipeline: Engaging the Church in Missionary Mobilization

Visit their website at www.threestrandpartners.org

The Wilsons love to travel and spend time outdoors. They currently live in Kansas City, Missouri.